Organizational Change Within the Social Security Administration:

An Assessment of the National Partnership for Reinvention Policy in the Southern Region

Dr. Wilson L. Triviño

Aura Free Press

Published by Aura Free Press, Marietta, Georgia USA

ISBN-10: 0974322636
ISBN-13: 978-09743226-3-6

Vita

Wilson Lubin Triviño, son of Lubin Angel Triviño and Aura (Rojas) Triviño, was born January 16, 1970, in Anaheim, California. He received his Bachelor of Arts from Kennesaw State University in 1992. In August 1994, he was awarded the degree of Master of Public Administration from Auburn University. In September 1994, he began to pursue a Doctor of Philosophy degree in Public Policy and Public Administration at Auburn University. During his time in graduate school, he taught American Government, Public Policy, and Public Administration in the Department of Political Science. In 1998, the author was invited by President Clinton to attend the White House Conference on Social Security. His past experience includes working with the Georgia House of Representatives, Georgia's Secretary of State, and as an executive assistant to the Southern Regional Commissioner of the Social Security Administration in Atlanta, Georgia. He has also been active in federal, state, and local political campaigns.

Dissertation Abstract

Organizational Change Within the Social Security Administration: An Assessment of the National

Partnership for Reinvention Policy in the Southern Region

Wilson Lubin Triviño
Doctor of Philosophy, August 5, 2002
(MPA, Auburn University, 1994)
(B.A., Kennesaw State University, 1992)

200 Typed Pages

Directed by Gerard Gryski

The purpose of this study was to assess the impact of the National Partnership for Reinvention

(NPR) policy within the Southern Region of the Social Security Administration (SSA). The NPR policy was

a part of the Clinton Administration's objective of "reinventing government" by creating a government that

"works better and costs less." By using the case study approach, the author examined the implementation

of NPR within the Southern Region of the SSA to determine if NPR created organizational change. This

dissertation brings attention and understanding to the important relationship between public policy

implementation, leadership styles, organizational culture and the mechanisms of change within public

institutions.

Acknowledgements

The author would first like to thank his parents, Lubin and Aura Triviño, whose love, support, and sacrifice has enabled him to complete this degree. Thanks are also due to his best friends and supporters: his brothers David, Miguel, and Daniel.

Sincere thanks are also extended to his dissertation committee, especially to his supervisor Dr. Gerard Gryski, who in addition to chairing the committee gave him invaluable advice and encouragement throughout, and to Dr. Gary Zuk, and Dr. Bradley Moody for their encouragement and professionalism in helping him to grow as an academic. Sincere appreciation is also extended to his mentor and friend, Gordon Sherman, an individual whose career and actions within the Social Security Administration exemplifies the best ideals of public service. A special recognition goes to the public servants within the Social Security Administration, whose everyday actions translate into a commitment to continue to provide a world-class service for their clients.

Style manual used: Style Manual for Political Science. The American Political Science Association, 1993 ed.

Computer software used: Microsoft Word 2000

Table of Contents

Vita..iii

Dissertation Abstract..v

Acknowledgements vii

Table of Contents...ix

Prologue..1

List of Figures 2

Chapter 1 Introduction..3

Chapter 2 Literature on Organizational Change...9

Chapter 3 The Social Security Administration (SSA)...................................35

Chapter 4 National Partnership for Reinvention (NPR)...............................67

Chapter 5 Research Methodology 87

Chapter 6 The Effective Implementation of National Partnership for Reinvention (NPR) within the Social Security Administration (SSA) 95

Chapter 7 Consequences of National Partnership for Reinventing Government (NPR) for the Southern Region of the Social Security Administration (SSA) 135

References 159

Appendix A Structured Interview 181

Appendix B Internal Memo with Agency Acronyms....................................183

About the Author...188

Prologue

Thanks for taking the time to review this study, it represents a culmination of almost a decade of work during my graduate study at Auburn University between 1993 and 2002. It is my unedited original dissertation. I have made no substantial changes to the text. I simply have taken it off the book shelf, dusted it off, and made it available to the world of ideas.

In 2002 I was the first Latino to get a doctorate in Political Science from Auburn University. I immensely enjoyed my years at Auburn University and this exercise taught me how to think as a scholar. I am appreciative for all that helped me through the process.

For those in a doctorate program or considering a one, the one piece of advice I want to share is to "do it". As my professor kept reminding me, "don't get it right, get it wrote". I see so many make the process more complicated than it should be and get sucked into ABD black hole. It is an internal struggle, and only YOU can finish it. No one will do it for you.

The years I spent studying the Social Security Administration were a fascinating examination of one of our nation's more successful and controversial programs. It reaffirmed my faith in our American system and that public service is a noble calling.

Leadership exist everywhere, but it takes one person willing to lead and have a vision for change. My mentor, Gordon Sherman, who served with distinction in government taught me that one person can make a difference. As a fellow Auburn man, I am always appreciative of his time and mentorship in making me the person I am today.

Implementing public policy is not as glamorous as the campaign rhetoric during the election season. But to get something done, we need an organization and program to do so. The Social Security policy has not been perfect but it has help millions of individuals sustain economic security. Political Science is really the study of people and how they work together to solve the big problems of our day. But often our policy makers prefer to "kick the can down the road" than to make the tough decisions today in order to ensure a better tomorrow.

I continue to be optimistic about our system and hope that this work will give you insight into one aspect of the nitty gritty complexity of implementing public policy. Large bureaucracies contain many challenges, but they are able embrace change and adapt to modern challenges. It takes visionaries to lead them.

I want to also thank to all those that continue to support my dreams. All those I consider family, especially my lawyer, best friend, and brother, David Triviño, Esq. who believes our best days lie ahead. His optimism is contagious and I value his counsel.

Franklin Delano Roosevelt said it best, "The dreams of today are the realities of tomorrow." Enjoy!

Dr. Wilson L. Triviño
August 18, 2015
The ABC Vision Innovation Center
Atlanta, Georgia USA

List of Figures

Figure 3.1   Social Security Administration (SSA) Regional Boundaries

Figure 3.2   SSA Organizational Chart

Figure 3.2   SSA Atlanta Regional Office Chart

Figure 3.3   SSA Field Facilities and Staff

Figure 4.1   Americans' Trust of the Federal Government

Figure 7.1   Southern Region Organizational Chart Pre-National Partnership for Reinvention (NPR)

Figure 7.2   Southern Regional Organizational Chart Post-NPR changes

Chapter 1 Introduction

Purpose

This dissertation explores whether implementation of the National Partnership for Reinvention (NPR) policy initiative by the Clinton Administration resulted in organizational change within the southern region of the Social Security Administration (SSA). It is the intent of this research, by the use of the case study method, to assess the dynamics found in implementation within the confines commonly found in public administration. This study examines the methods and management approaches that illustrate administrative capacity to create institutional change. In addition, this study focuses on the policy and administrative complexities that challenge Social Security policy makers and public servants as they grapple with growing administrative and political pressures. To these ends, the first part of the study details the policy making process in the SSA, identifying key actors and policy advocates who have advanced Social Security policy. The second part illustrates administrative approaches that were employed in the management and implementation of the NPR policy within the confines of the SSA. By briefly exploring the SSA and the NPR policy, this chapter outlines the organization of this dissertation, and its significance of this study in the field of public administration. The Social Security Administration (SSA)

"Social security" in its broadest sense can be taken as the "security of the whole society" and could include not only physical and mental security but also even spiritual security. Therefore, this broad definition of social security creates a challenge because of the many interpretations of what constitutes social security (Armstrong, 1932; Epstein, 1968; Rubinow, 1934). The idea of social security, however, encompasses many other areas related to education, health care, and economic security. More commonly viewed as retirement income replacement insurance, the Social Security program deals with other areas for Americans. In the United States, Social Security refers to the benefits provided by the Old Age, Survivors, and Disability Insurance system (OASDI) and the health benefits provided by the Medicare program and the Social Security Acts (Meyers, 1993, p. 6). Today, 92 percent of Americans sixty-five and over are receiving Social Security retirement benefits. If it were not for this program, the poverty rate for the elderly would be over fifty percent (Sherman, 1998, p. 26). Since its inception sixty years ago, Social Security has been and continues to be one of government's most successful and controversial programs (Kingson and Schulz, 1997; Graetz and Mashaw, 1999; Schieber and Shoven, 1999).

The National Partnership for Reinventing (NPR) Government

SSA is a complex federal bureaucracy that provides a basic level of social insurance for most working Americans. The Social Security program has evolved significantly since its inception in the 1935 Social Security Act (49 Stat., 620). In its development, the agency has experienced constant challenges from the shifting demands and needs of public and elected officials. NPR was focused on making government "work better and cost less," arising from the public's critical view of the federal government (Gore, 1993). This policy was an attempt to facilitate change within a federal bureaucracy that was rooted in the industrial age toward one that existed in the global information age. This policy could be categorized as a part of a much larger continuing focus on federal government reform. This particular reform originated in the 1992 Clinton presidential campaign and has gone through several phases, all of which have been focused on how to bring organizational change to the federal government. This research examines how it specifically influenced SSA. This study is limited to the examination of NPR Policy in the Southern Regional of the SSA at the regional level. This policy is a government-wide program and has operated since 1993, yet this study examines only the influences on one region of the SSA.

NPR is focused on making government "work better and cost less," to be achieved by implementing the initial objectives of: (1) Cutting Red Tape, (2) Putting Customers First, (3) Empowering Employees to

Get Results, (4) Cutting Back to Basics (Gore, 1993). This research attempts to see if this policy created organizational change in the Southern region of the SSA. The following determine organizational change: (1) Did the administrative structure and decision making change within the Southern Region? (2) Was the language used in internal documents within the Southern Region influenced by this policy? (3) Did the recognition of success by NPR criteria result in real improvement of services provided by the SSA? (4) Did the administrators in the Southern Region perceive NPR as a real change in the way in which SSA operated?

I became involved with the SSA in the summer of 1994 when invited by Southern Regional Commissioner Gordon Sherman to attend an internal SSA regional management conference in Atlanta. Continuing that relationship with the agency, I interned in the Southern Regional Offices in Atlanta during the summer and holiday breaks between 1996-1999 as part of the regional office staff. Gordon Sherman facilitated my gaining access to the internal dynamics of the implementation of the Social Security program. The interest in the NPR stemmed from conversations in 1997 with Social Security Commissioner Shirley Chater and her continued focus on the NPR Policy. This focal point stirred my interest to pursue an in depth analysis on organizational change within the Southern Region.

Significance of this Study

This research focuses on how organizational change within the SSA occurs, specifically assessing the impact of the NPR initiative within the Southern Region. The questions addressed are: (1) The National Partnership for Reinvention Policy initiative had an impact on the goals that define the service provided by the Southern Region of the SSA; (2) If organizational change in the Southern Region of the SSA was a product of the NPR Policy Initiative; (3) The service provided by the Southern Region of the SSA, defined in terms of its formal goals, was altered substantially by the NPR initiative.

Why is Social Security worthy of exploration? The SSA is a premier public organization that has accumulated a rich history of meeting the economic security needs of all working Americans. SSA has been very successful; in its sixty-five years history, the agency has never missed a payment to its beneficiaries.

The agency is very cost effective because it provides services at an administrative cost of less than one cent from every tax dollar received (SSA, 2000a). Since its inception, the Social Security program has always been a politically controversial program and has had to adapt to the changing needs of society. However, the agency has reached a level of institutional maturity.

NPR's focus is on making the federal government "work better and cost less," which can be construed as a part of the continuous effort to enable government to reform government. This research is relevant because it speaks to core issues of public administration: policy implementation, leadership style, organizational culture, and organizational change. Finally, this research is important because it yields a better understanding of how applied public policy works and how planning and implementation public people's perception of the policy process.

Method of this Study

A systematic case study analysis with theory-grounded approach is used to address the types and degrees of change affected by NPR. This method synthesizes interviews, documents analysis, and first-hand observations of the SSA and the implementation of NPR. These three data sources allow a triangulated analysis of the research questions. Ground-theory is theory that is discovered or generated from data rather than being abstract and deductive (Glaser & Strauss, 1967; Yin, 1989). This methodology is most appropriate to distinguish the personal frames of reference of those officials who are ambiguously situated. McCracken states: "The purpose of the qualitative interview is not to discover how many, and what kinds of people share certain characteristic. It is to gain access to the cultural categories and assumptions according to which one construes the world" (1988, p. 17)." The data were collected while on the executive staff in the office of the regional commissioner of the southern region of SSA for the summers between 1996 and 1999. This position facilitated access throughout the SSA as well as the NPR staff.

Organization of the Dissertation

There are seven chapters in this study. Two is a review of literature in areas pertinent to this study: organizational change, leadership styles, organizational culture, and studying public policy implementation. Chapter Three presents a brief overview of the evolution of the SSA and how the agency changed as a reaction to the political, bureaucratic, and environmental pressures. Chapter Four addresses the development and evolution of government reform and how this historical development influenced the creation of the NPR. This chapter also looks into this policy's relationship with the SSA. The theoretical considerations and methodology used in this study are addressed in Chapter Five. Chapter Six and Seven deals with the research findings, summary, and conclusion.

Chapter 2 Literature on Organizational Change

" There is nothing more difficult to take in hand, more perilous to conduct, or more uncertain in its success, than to take the lead in the introduction of a new order of things."
-Niccoló Machiavelli, *The Prince*

Organizations exist for a reason. They provide a service, produce a product, or implement a public policy. They exist in many forms and are found in every aspect of human civilization. To achieve an understanding of their dynamics, one must ask, "What do organizations do and how well do they do it?" Organizations serve a purpose, but they do not exist in a vacuum. In the much larger universe of which they are a part, both internal and external forces exert an influence on them. The literature within the field of organizational theory is vast and wide-ranging. This literature review explores and defines in specific terms the on-going debate and conclusions reached so far by scholars engaged in the study of organizations. This chapter reviews the literature concerning organizational theory in order to apply it to the topic of this dissertation: Did the National Partnership for Reinvention (NPR) policy influence organizational change within the Southern Region of the Social Security Administration (SSA)? This chapter begins with an overview of the significance of the problem addressed to further our understanding of public institutions. It explains the life cycles of organizations and the differences between public and private organizations. Furthermore it narrows the focus by explaining why the variables of organizational change, leadership styles, and organizational culture were used and provides an in-depth discussion of the literature of each. Being an implementation study, reviews of different approaches to public policy are discussed as well. SSA is a large federal agency that has a significant impact on the quality of life for a substantial number of citizens. SSA administers the largest federal government program, accounting for over one fourth of all federal government expenditures, and is directed by a specific mission defined by agency wide goals. In this context, NPR is an important new federal initiative designed to help federal agencies become more effective and efficient.

When studying large organizations like the SSA, it is logical to approach such investigations with a point of reference from the existing body of work on organizations. This literature encompasses a broad perspective of organizations and this study focuses specifically on the areas of organizational change, leadership styles, and organizational culture.

Defining Variables

This study explores the question of whether the NPR Policy initiative has had a discernible impact on the services provided by the Atlanta Region of SSA. If so, this impact is likely to have been accomplished through significant and appropriate organizational changes. This study centers on the variables of organizational change, leadership styles, and organizational culture because they are best suited to explore the dynamics of the focus of this dissertation. Organizational change was chosen because it is the central theme of this dissertation. Previous scholars have debated what works and what does not work in facilitating effective change. Secondly, leadership styles was chosen because each organization moves in a direction; effective leaders are able to set the course. Finally, organizations are human institutions that reflect the values placed on them by the individuals within them. Organizational culture is explored to see how its history and value system creates a particular organizational culture. More specifically, in dealing with change, the culture of an organization can either facilitate or hinder successful change. This is particularly evident in SSA, as the agency is a service-oriented organization composed of thousands of employees from every part of the United States from which it has developed its own particular institutional values.

Before exploring the individual parts that make up an organization, we first must understand that the composition of an organization is not static. SSA has been in existence for sixty-five years and is now a mature public institution. In public institutions, the life of an organization goes through stages of development comparable to a life cycle (Downs, 1967: Kaufman, 1976; Grafton, 1975). These stages not only influence the internal mechanics of the organization, but also bear a strong relationship to the surrounding environment and the type of individuals who are attracted to become a part of it (Maccoby, 1976).

A common comparison to this evolution of organizations is that of a living organism, which undergoes birth, maturity, and death (Mayo, 1933; Kaufman, 1976; Morgan, 1986). This cycle is a continual process filled with changes and experiences. Most of the research published on organizational life cycles has focused on this process, from conception to eventual decline (Kimberly, Miles, and Associates 1980; Cameron, Sutton, & Whetten, 1988).

The large organizations that dominate today's world have not always existed. Contrary to popular belief, longevity of any organization is the exception rather than the rule; most organizations disintegrate after a relatively short period of time (Hage, 1980). History shows that world civilizations have disappeared and been replaced in a never ending cycle (Toynbee, 1947). Government bureaucracy is commonly viewed as eternal and difficult to change, but public sector organizations are always changing. For example, many of the programs created during the explosive period of the New Deal no longer exist today (Kaufman, 1976). Over the course of its sixty-five year existence, SSA has had to adapt continually in order to keep pace with its ever-shifting social, political, and economic environment. This program has been highly successful in meeting its own objectives and continuing to provide economic security for American workers. The SSA has evolved to become a mature public institution that is both highly political and highly bureaucratic. In an age where politicians use political rhetoric to shun "big government," Social Security has expanded its responsibilities. The growth of the agency is best explained by Gryski, (1981), "government is playing a larger role in anticipating problems and initiating programs to deal with them in addition to responding to obvious problems is another source of growth. In a very real sense, the federal government is doing- albeit imperfectly – what society wants done" (p. 235). Social Security was created to mirror society's changing challenges and this research addresses the question; Has the NPR policy created real organizational change within SSA? Anthony Downs (1967) applied the life cycle analogy directly to public bureaus. He argues that most government bureaus pass through an eight-stage development process, even though the amount of time spent on each may differ considerably. They are:

1. Agency birth

2. Early dominance by advocates or zealots

3. Struggle for autonomy

4. Struggle for support

5. Rapid growth

6. Deceleration effect

7. Age lump (crisis of continuity)

8. Death

The inception, or birth, may occur in four different ways. First, a charismatic leader brings together a group of followers, who then transforms themselves into a bureau. Second, a group of individuals perceives a need to carry out a specific function, and creates a bureau to assist them in this quest. Third, a new bureau can be created as the result of an existing bureau giving up some of its functions. Finally, a bureau may be created through policy entrepreneurship. In their early stages, bureaus are dominated by advocates or zealots and experience a rapid rate of growth. If they do not immediately receive outside support, the bureau may be faced with an early demise.

In order to survive, bureaus must gain support from both groups they serve and existing government bureaus. The ever-changing environment encourages them to seek stability even as they are struggling to survive. As the bureau expands and grows, the average level of talent within it declines. In the early stages, highly-talented individuals join the bureau, but this effect diminishes as the bureau gets larger. The natural shift in recruitment has a cumulative effect, which Downs labels the *deceleration effect*. At this stage, conservatives dominate the organization, seeking to enhance status or job promotion prospects for those already employed. Finally, if the bureau fails to perform the social functions deemed necessary by its clients, or if the functions of the bureau are taken over by another bureau, death is a possibility.

A fascinating and important controversy focuses on whether or not there are real distinctions between private or public organizations. These distinctions often have been vague in the literature and scholars caution against oversimplification when distinguishing between public and private management. Some experts argue that there are no real differences between the two (Baldwin, 1987; Bozeman, 1987), while others have spelled out perceived differences (Rainey, 1976). This section addresses the differences and similarities found between public and private sector organizations.

Much of the work on organization change has been on business organizations, but this work also applies to public organizations (Van de Ven, 1981; Quinn and Cameron, 1983). In the private sector, free market forces make it possible for bureaucracies to change at a faster pace. However, this does not always happen. There are many large and profitable companies that seemed invincible but have failed due the shifting needs of consumers, obsolete products, and so forces these companies ceased to exist (Bennis, 1997).

Public institutions are constantly facing change, ranging from shifts in political leadership to new environmental demands, and often are resistant to it. In public bureaucracies, change can be costly, troublesome, unfamiliar, threatening, and difficult to understand and accomplish (Zaltman, Duncan, and Holbeck, 1977). The political system produces continual shifts in emphasis among several goals, creating change that the executive branch representatives and executive leadership must deal with while simultaneously maintaining an acceptable level of politically-neutral competence (Golembiewski, 1972).

The major challenge for public managers is to discover ways to overcome the obstacles preventing such participation and flexibility amid the political complexities and accountability pressures in government. Public sector managers are handicapped because they are not as flexible as their private sector counterparts due to the limitations imposed by the Constitution or legally binding authorities. This creates an environment with multiple actors, all of whom have access to multiple authorities. Different interests and reward structures often compound the problem. In public sector organizations, there are sets of complex administrative hierarchies which are at times fragmented and weakened by competing affiliations. Administrative officials may have stronger ties to congressional allies and stronger commitments to their programs than to the top executives in their departments or to the President. The weak linkage between career civil service and politically appointed executives produces a problem of diffuse authority (Rainey, 1991).

Understanding the present stage of SSA in its organizational life and the constant conflicting demands leads to a better understanding of this public institution. Contrary to the market demands of the private sector, SSA as a public institution possesses a more complex responsibility to social public policy. The following sections review the ideas from the literature to research in the areas of organizational change, leadership styles, and organizational culture.

Organizational Change

A great deal of the research of organization theorists has been on the topic of change (Galaskiewicz and Bielefeld, 1998). One of the greatest opportunities for development, both for an organization as a whole and for its staff as individuals, occurs during times of crisis and change (Rogers et. al, 1985). Change is inevitable for individuals, organizations, and society (March and Simon, 1958). Simply scanning the environment shows how the factors influence these shifts caused by technology, needs, resource availability and political control of government. Change is endemic, but it is frequently unpredictable and uncontrollable and the rate of change appears to be increasing. If this constant state of flux is unsettling for individuals, it is doubly so for organizations (Poole et al, 2000). Change is little understood, and there are few recognized ways to cope with it from an organizational perspective. Change disturbs equilibrium and disrupts relationships within an environment. Change comes in many forms, and not all are beneficial - change always involves costs as well as benefits (Cohen et.al., 1972). Even if change is ultimately beneficial, organizations, like individuals, frequently resist and resent it. The inevitability of change and the necessity for organizations to adapt to it make it one of the most important concerns of contemporary organizational theory (Utterback, 1994, Kanter, 1995).

Organizations experience shifts over time and may need to change significantly each time. The need to change is the need to grow. Having the ability to adapt constantly to a shifting environment enables organizations to survive (Senge, 1995). A sprawling literature addresses organizational change and innovation, with much of it, including the elaborate sub-field of organizational development, focused on how to change organizations for the better. Organizations change constantly (Meyer, 1979). Successful organizational change is not easy or simple. There are many variables to consider, as there are people within organizations. To present only one model or theory of organizational change is misleading and discredits the abundance of good research. Contemporary research on implementing change into organizations suggests that there are significant factors that influence success at organizational change.

Modern organization theories discuss three primary factors or contingencies that determine the appropriateness of various organization structures (Weber, 1946; Chandler, 1962; Woodward, 1965; Lawrence and Lorsch, 1967; Thompson, 1967; Mintzberg, 1979). These theories and recent empirical findings indicate that strong relationships exist between an organization's environment, its technical systems, its strategic actions, the appropriateness of its structure, and its performance and general effectiveness. In general, current evidence indicates that organizations operating in the same environment, executing similar strategic actions, and employing the same technical systems and resources are more or less effective depending upon the appropriateness of their structures, including communication and information systems (Galbraith, 1977; Mintzberg, 1979). This theory suggests that the existence of new environments, new technical systems, and strategic actions requires new organizational structures.

Typically, the concept of organizational change deals with organization-wide change, as opposed to smaller changes such as adding a new member of staff or modifying the responsibilities of an existing member of staff (O'Toole, 1995). Examples of organization-wide change might include a change in mission, a restructure in operations (e.g., restructuring to self-managed teams, layoffs, etc.), and on introduction of new technology, mergers, major collaborations, or "rightsizing." Some experts refer to change as organizational transformation. Often the term designates a fundamental and radical reorientation in the way the organization operates. Terreberry hypothesizes that "organizational change" is largely externally induced (1968, p. 610).

Conceptually, how can we arrive at other change strategies? Given the highly interdependent nature of organizations, the problem of change can be bewildering. Simplification becomes both desirable and inevitable. Leavitt has selected four interacting variables: task, technology, people, and structure. The task variable is seen as the primary output variable, while people, technology, and structure are seen as potential strategies for organizational change. Each approach to organizational change differs in terms of point of entry, the primary lever of change, and the causal sequence of change (Leavitt, 1965).

The literature on organizational change can be roughly divided into two areas of either a structural approach or a people-based approach (Zaleznick, 1965; Barnes, 1967; Hornstein, 1971) The structured school of thought can be traced to the scientific management and administrative science movements early in the 20th century. Stimulated by F.W. Taylor and Heri Fayol, the scientific approach was directed at discovering the best way to organize. With their closed-system perspective, the thrust of organizational change was direct and if the rules of organizing were followed, the question of organizational change need never come up (Maisse, 1965). Since Mayo, however, the folly of the simplistic notions and confident principles of scientific management have been exposed (Mayo, 1933). Scientific management did work indeed for certain kinds of organizations, but the principles were extended to apply to all organizations. This school's closed system perspective has been abandoned and a view emphasizing the organization in constant commerce with and potential dependence on its environment has taken its place (Katz and Kahn, 1966; Thompson, 1967).

Change is seen as a continual process of structural adaptation (Sayles, 1962; Meyer, 1978). Since Taylor and Fayol, structural orientation has treated organizations as interdependent systems embedded in an uncertain environment. More examples of this structural approach to change are field studies, which include Blau (1955), Morse and Reimer (1956), Lawrence (1958), Guest (1962). These researchers make a convincing case for the structural approach. The problem then becomes when, and under what conditions, does structural change lead to the desired behavioral and organizational change? What are the effects of differing environments and technologies on group influence and individual predisposition through the process of change?

The other major approach to organizational change is the people-based approach (Leavitt, 1965). This approach also is referred to in the literature by terms such as power equalization (Strauss, 1964; Leavitt, 1965; Shepard, 1965), eupsychian management (Maslow, 1965), planned change (Barnes, 1967), organizational renewal (Lippit, 1969) and participation (Mann and Neff, 1961; Likert, 1961, 1967). All refer to a set of efforts that effect organizational change through changes in the people who staff the organization.

People-based approaches attempt to change organizations by first influencing the attitudes, values, and norms within the individual members of the organization, leading them to follow the new path. Structure is believed to follow. While usually aware of the technological and structural constraints, these researchers are mainly preoccupied with people as the primary lever for change. They believe that an organization can be changed by focusing on the individual's point of view (Herzberg, 1966).

Many scholars argue that the problems with American organizations are managerial. For instance, Hersey and Blanchard (1993) contend that today's professional managers have the wrong priorities, tending to be oriented toward finance and short term profits rather than innovation. Reich (1987) claims that these managers have resorted to "paper entrepreneurism," the sorting of numbers, as opposed to true entrepreneurship. Some have argued that American organizations lack champions who are able to implement ideas and create results. For instance, Peters and Waterman (1982) argue that excellence in the organizations they studied is related to a combination of a champion and an organizational structure that allows the champion to succeed. They note that poorly performing firms lack one or both of these requirements.

Even though many writers are suggesting that organizations should be more entrepreneurial, they give little guidance on how this can be achieved. Simply arguing that organizations need to be more entrepreneurial neglects the research that has been reported suggesting that entrepreneurs and bureaucracy do not go well together (Chandler, 1962). If organizations are to be more entrepreneurial in the future, managers and researchers must solve the problem of how to relate the entrepreneur and entrepreneurial functions to the operations of large, bureaucratic organizations. One fundamental step in this direction is understanding the basic differences between entrepreneurs, entrepreneurial organizations, and today's large bureaucratic organizations.

18

One way that organizations are able to change is that they can become so-called "learning organizations" that are better able to adapt to the ever-shifting demands of the environment in which they operate. These shifts can cause organizations to enter into a new paradigm and change their entire operational focus. In recent management literature, organizational learning has attracted growing interests among both students and practitioners of management (Senge, 1995). Managers are competing in quickly changing environments, venturing into new organizational forms and relationships, and facing mounting pressures to deliver value for money in the public sector. They are led to ask why some organizations display faster and more efficient learning than others, and how their investment in training and developing individuals can be transferred into learning by the organization as a whole. These practitioner concerns lead to academic interest and pose theoretical challenges because they cross disciplines, levels of analyses and organizational cultures (Argyris, 1996). Argyris presents an impressive source of ideas that adds to our understanding of organizational learning, arguing that the more effectively organizations can learn, the more likely they will be able to correct errors and be able to innovate successfully.

Another method of monitoring organizational effectiveness created by change is by analysis. Poister and Streib (1994) provide empirical evidence concerning the use of performance management strategies in government. They find that program evaluation, forecasting, performance monitoring, employee involvement efforts, and strategic planning are among the most frequently used approaches in creating effective organizations. Tools that have been developed more recently have not yet been widely adopted. Eadie (1983) discusses the application of strategic planning to government organizations. Through strategic planning, organizations and communities develop new goals, update their missions, and create a shared commitment among leaders and stakeholders for current and future endeavors. Kaufman (1981) lays out some lessons that public agencies have learned in applying strategic planning, including the creation of a schematic road map. Halachmi (1991) observes that while strategic planning often adopts a comprehensive and agency-wide perspective, many changes are incremental and made by sub-units within the organization.

Organizational change may mean different things to different organizations, but in most cases what the leadership considers important effectively determines what the organization does well.

To develop more flexibility in public agencies, trust within organizations must be enhanced. Unfortunately, because of an out dated bureaucratic model of government, government agencies face major deficits of trust (Carnevale, 1995). This deficit may be overcome by competent public administrators who foster loyalty within the bureaucracy. Unlike their private sector counterparts, public institutions are often given less credit for innovation and lack credibility when handling challenges (Osborne and Gabler, 1993). Their environment fosters an attitude of antagonism to change rather than inviting new opportunities.

The culture, climate, and age of an organization are major factors determining its willingness and ability to change. The culture of an organization comprises the shared beliefs, attitudes, and values of its members, which determine the organization's norms of behavior. The more widely and firmly held a set of values, the more difficult they will be to change. A change that conflicts with basic values about what the organization does or how it should do it will meet with strong resistance (Stewart and Garson, 1983). The factors identified, which may consist of a wide range of internal and external forces, may necessitate change within an organization. External forces of change include factors such as government laws and regulations, advances in technology, and social and economic change. Internal forces of change are generally characterized as ineffective technology, staff, or task and administrative structures (Leavitt, 1965).

In 1947, Kurt Lewin described the process of changing individual behavior as involving three steps: unfreezing, moving, and refreezing. The same steps are involved in organizational change. Unfreezing behavior means disturbing the equilibrium of the organization sufficiently to make the organization ready and willing to change. The final step, refreezing, integrates the change that has been made into the organization's culture and behavior.

Two basically contrasting strategies exist for implementing change: top-down and power equalization. Top-down change strategy is characterized by the unilateral use of power. "Change is implemented through an emphasis on the authority of a man's hierarchical position, there the definition and solution to the problem at hand tends to be specified by the upper echelons and directed through formal and impersonal control mechanisms" (Greiner, 1972, p. 52). Changes are decreed by those at the top of the organization; implementation frequently involves the replacement of individuals in key positions and structural modifications that change the relationships of subordinates working in the organization. Power equalization strategies involve shared power, in which authority is still vested to those at the top but there is also interaction and sharing of power at lower levels (Greiner, 1967). Obviously, proponents of participatory management are convinced that power equalization strategies, particularly the shared power approach, are more effective than a top-down strategy. Theoretically, a shared power strategy should increase an understanding of and commitment to the changes, improve the quality of the changes, enrich workers' jobs, and encourage democracy in the workplace (Drucker, 1985). Some examples of these attempts to bring change into specifically federal agencies can include reorganizations, shifts in political appointees, and programs that incorporate the latest craze such as Total Quality Management, Zero Base Budgets, or Reinventing Government.

Change in the federal bureaucracy has always been a huge undertaking.
Franklin D. Roosevelt, who was a very effective President, vented his frustrations:

> The Treasury is so large and far-flung and ingrained in its practices that I find it almost impossible to get the action and results I want. . . But the Treasury is not to be compared with the State Department. You should go through the experience of trying to get any changes in the thinking, policy, and action of the career diplomats and then you'd know what a real problem was. But the Treasury and the State Department are nothing compared with the Navy. The admirals are really something to cope with - and I should know. To change anything in the Navy is like punching a feather bed. You punch it with your right hand and you punch it with your left hand until you are finally exhausted, and then you find the damn bed just as it was before you started punching (Haass, 1999, p.5).

The relevant literature focuses on how and why organizations deal with change. These changes are brought about because of the shifting environmental demands or a continual need to improve efficiency. In the case of SSA, its responsibility is to send out the right check for the right amount to the right person every month. However, this is not as easy as it may seem. First of all, there is a need to implement the program and make sure it is adjudicated equitably. SSA is a very bureaucratic agency at a mature stage of its organizational life cycle which can hinder change. Yet, SSA's changes come from different sources, such as a continual shift of appointed personnel by new presidential administrations, the shifting demographics of its core constituencies, and the introduction of new technologies into its well-established practices. Effective change cannot occur without good leadership and the next section moves into understanding and defining the role of leadership.

Leadership

An organization usually produces what its leadership considers to be important (Sherman, 1999). Organizations are not a simple set of squares and arrows in an organizational chart; they are composed of individuals who create a complex network of interdependent relationships. The challenge for an effective leader is to identify these relationships and take them into account. Leaders must become aware of all these factors and work to create an environment that meets the objectives of their organization (Bennis, 1997).

The word "leadership" is a relatively recent addition to the English language. It only has been in use for around two hundred years, although the term "leader" from which it was derived appeared as early as 1300 A.D (Stogdill, 1974). Most concepts of leadership imply that at some point one or more group members can be identified as a leader according to some observable difference between that person and other group members, who are referred to as "followers" or subordinates." Definitions of leadership usually share a common denominator, the assumption that it is a group phenomenon involving an interaction between two or more persons (Bennis, 1989).

Leadership is an important component in developing useful and potential organizations, so fostering effective leadership is a vital concern (Burns, 1978). The success of an organization often is attributed to the possession of good leadership. The necessary traits have been explored extensively and have been shown to contribute substantially to the performance of an organization (Yukl, 1981). Although the word itself is a relatively recent addition to the lexicon, leadership is one of the oldest areas that has been studied in an attempt to understand relationships. Leadership depends on the influence that individuals within organizations have, and this authority has a major influence on the dynamics within any organization (Cleveland, 1985).

In reviewing the literature on leadership, "close to 3,000 books and articles have been published on the subject of leadership, mostly within the past three decades," notes business writer Richard Luecke (1994). In spite of this endeavor, the concept of leadership continues to elude us, constantly reemerging in another form to taunt us with its complexity. An endless proliferation of terms has been invented to deal with it, but still the concept is not clear (Bennis, 1959). Stogdill (1974) writes that there are as many definitions of leadership as there are persons who have attempted to define it. Leadership has been defined in terms of individual traits, behavior, influence over other people, interaction patterns, role relationships, occupation of administrative positions, and perceptions of others regarding legitimacy of influence. Stogdill, after an exhaustive survey of the literature, concludes that, "leadership is not a matter of passive status, or of the mere possession of some combination of traits. It appears to be a working relationship among members of a group, in which the leader acquires status through active participation and demonstration of his capacity for carrying cooperative tasks through to completion" (p. 25).

The other concept, functional leadership, emphasizes the circumstances under which groups of people integrate and organize their activities toward objectives, and upon the way in which that integration and organization are achieved. Thus, the leadership function is analyzed and understood in terms of a dynamic relationship. A leader may acquire followers, or a group of people may create a leader. The significant aspects of the process can be understood only in dynamic relationship terms. Evidence and speculation to date make it appear that this functional or operational conception of leadership provides the most useful approach (Tead, 1935).

A large part of the enduring preoccupation of Americans with leadership is the ambivalence with which they regard it. The yearning for decisive leaders, coupled with the apprehension that they might upset the balance between power and liberty, has made Americans more adept at demanding leadership than at embracing it (Wilson, 1885). Weber began the modern inquiry into the role of leadership as the world trended toward rationalization in every sphere of society. Weber identified three ideal types of leadership: the rational legal, the rational authoritarian, and the charismatic. The charismatic leaders were identified as those who were best suited to counter the dispiriting effects of life in a overly-bureaucratic and rationalistic world, the iron cage of modernity. This type of leader would be able to instill his or her followers with a sense of mission and moral purpose that a thoroughly demystified society no longer provides (Weber, 1946).

James MacGregor Burns (1978) synthesizes twenty five years of studying political leadership into a model that borrows heavily from social psychology, offering a psychological theory of leadership which is based on an exchange of motives and values. Power and leadership are viewed not as "things," but as relationships. "We must analyze power in the context of human motives and physical constraints. If we can come to grips with these aspects of power, we can hope to comprehend the true nature of leadership- a venture far more intellectually daunting than the study of naked power" (1978, p.11). Burns identifies two types of leadership: transactional and transforming. The essence of the leader-follower relationship is the interaction of persons with different levels of motives and power potential, including skill, in pursuit of a common, or at least joint, purpose. However, the interaction takes two fundamentally different forms. Transactional leadership is based on an exchange, which may be either economic or political, between leaders and followers, but the participant motivations remain unchanged. Transactional leadership can be viewed as the "stuff" of everyday political exchange. Transforming leadership is moral leadership combined with a fusion of purpose and vision between leaders and followers. Such leadership comes when one or more persons engage with others in such a way that leaders and followers raise one another to higher levels of motivation and morality. Gandhi is the example given. Burns cites examples of executive, legislative, and party leadership: "Party leadership is transactional, but it has vast transforming potential" (1978, p. 343). He goes on to conclude: "Executive leadership, to produce intended real change, must be solidly founded on power and principle" (1978, p. 397). Yet, Bass (1985) argues that Burns created a wholly artificial distinction between transactional and transformational leaders. Far from being antithetical, these two types of leadership can exist in the same person or, by the same token, not exist at all in a leader.

Organizations are human institutions and may take either a mechanistic approach or a more humanistic one (McGregor, 1960). The objectives of an organization have a direct link to the individual needs and the higher organizational needs (MacGregor, 1966). Having the ability to create a vision and follow through and directing individuals to apply this vision, enables a leader to be effective in accomplishing his objectives (Kouzes and Posner, 1987). A set of beliefs and values can be instrumental in embedding a system of organizational values (Barnard, 1938; Selznick, 1957). Strong leadership within an organization is a way through which the organization can be improved.

As time passes, it has become clear that democracy is dependent on bureaucracy and the role of administrative officials. There have been calls for leadership to be reintroduced into the administration of public bureaucracies (Wilson, 1989). The role of leadership in accomplishing any task is to set a direction, create a vision for the organization, align people in such a way that they can implement that vision, and then communicate the vision to them, motivating and inspiring them to attain that vision. Management responsibility's to plan and budget for the direction set by the leader. The organization and its staff must create the organizational structure needed to implement the plan, control activities and solve problems in achieving the desired goal (Kaufman 1960; Drucker, 1985). The skills of public leadership are not the skills of management or manipulation, but rather the skills required to assist individuals and groups to realize their fullest potential and deal with change. Leadership, in this view, is educative, concerned primarily with power, and is rarely enduring (Denhardt, 1981).

Leadership has been a much debated concept and is more than a broad definition. The task of implementing NPR within SSA is a big undertaking, but effective administrators within the agency are able to facilitate the success of the program. What this study sets out to accomplish is to discover what qualities in the administrators enabled NPR to make a difference within SSA. Because organizations are human, they are heavily influenced by the composition of their membership. Each organization's culture and value system is shaped by its history and the next section explores organizational culture.

Organizational Culture

To comprehend any organization fully, the culture within the organization must be understood. The study of organizational culture was created by anthropologists in order to describe those elements of a social system that were, in many senses, the least changeable aspects of that system (Kilmann et. al, 1985). The use of culture can be traced back to the field of archeology (Schein, 1985). Culture is to the organization what personality is to the individual - a hidden, yet unifying, force that provides meaning, direction, and mobilization (Kilmann et. al, 1985). The members of the organization shape its personality, which transcends their individual motives and concerns. By studying its culture, one can deduce by observation what is going on within the organization based on the interactions and relationships between the actors inside the organization. The real challenge is to be able to measure this intangible aspect of the organization by an analysis of the language, artifacts, and values found within the institution.

Understanding the culture of an organization is another way in which social scientists can put on a different set of "lenses" to observe how the organization operates (Ott, 1989). Schein's (1985) concept of culture puts the burden on corporate leadership, especially the founders' vision(s) of the organization. Of special importance to Schein is the idea of leader-member, leader-group, and inter-group relationships in organizations, since what happens between the members of a group is the source of culture. Using an alternative approach, Schein attempts to conceptualize three levels of organizational culture: the basic underlying assumptions, artifacts, and values and beliefs (Schein, 1981, 1984, 1985).

One important point to understand is that within an organization, a simple snapshot of the hierarchy and structure does not necessarily capture an adequate image of the environment. By being a strong force, the culture supports the survival of the organization by indoctrinating new members, maintaining values, and extending the effective lifetime of the organization. Ott (1989) attempts to characterize the different experiences witnessed within the organization in addition to addressing the growth in interest in organizational culture. In an alternative approach, Dennison (1990) uses the case study method in an attempt to uncover the characteristics possessed by an effective organization. Dennison traces the increasing interest in organization culture in the 1980s. Since 1980, several authors have examined the relationship between the way an organization deals with change and survival issues and the many cultures that exist within it. These studies contribute greatly to our understanding of organizational culture in a highly dynamic world by exposing the delicate intricacies found within organizations (Schein, 1985).

Another means toward understanding the culture within an organization is through the examination of artifacts, which include material and nonmaterial objects that intentionally or unintentionally communicate information about the organization's technology, beliefs, values, assumptions, and ways of doing things. Artifacts can be annual reports, internal memos, promotional brochures, sales pieces, physical layouts or arrangements of offices, company cars, and items of dress. Organizational language, jargon, metaphors, stories, myths, and jokes also can be artifacts, and patterns of administrative behavior and organizational leadership are beginning to be described as cultural artifacts rather than expressions of individual leadership style or patterns of behavior (Sergiovanni and Corbally, 1984). Organizational charts are artifacts that are symbolic representations used to satisfy the expectations of important constituencies inside and outside the organization, such as environmental protection groups, minority protection groups, and women's advocacy groups. They are rarely working descriptions of reality (Ott, 1989).

In developing an understanding of the organizational culture, there are several key areas that can be analyzed to show the culture within the organization. For example, it is often useful to examine the language used and the stories passed from the tenured members of the organization to new members.

Culture is the force behind the tangible and observable aspects of any organization, and it involves the social energy that moves people to act.

Organization culture is impacting because it sets the direction, persuasiveness and strength of the organization (Kilmann et. al, 1985). "Strong" cultures are somehow more likely to be associated with effectiveness than "weak" cultures, and a strong culture can be deliberately created (Ouchi, 1981; Deal and Kennedy, 1982; Peters and Waterman, 1982).

Some view public bureaus as complex linguistic games, as cultural constructions rather than the objective realities we assume we perceive, or as "psychic prisons" and instruments of class domination (Burrell and Morgan, 1979; Denhart, 1981). Of particular importance is the understanding of the culture found in public institutions, which tends to attract individuals who are concerned with public service (Wilson, 1989). The environment of civil service regulations creates a culture that frowns on innovation and supports focusing on the process rather than the final outcome (Osborne and Plastri, 1997). This perspective promotes a culture in public institutions that is cautious, bureaucratic, and resistant to change. However, because of the vast complexities of the federal bureaucracies, there are pockets of innovation and change (Peters and Waterman, 1982; Kanter, 1989).

The literature indicates that to understand any organization an examination of its culture fills in the gaps. In any organization, there are important keys to unlocking the secrets of the organizational culture, such as its values, artifacts, and language. My experience as an intern within SSA facilitated an immersion into the internal dynamics of this large bureaucracy. The research clearly points to this understanding a means to understand the implementation of NPR within SSA. Because this research is a study in public policy, an understanding of approaches to studying public policy needs to be addressed and the next section does this.

Studying Public Policy Implementation

Research reveals that there are least three generations of evolutionary changes in the public policy implementation literature to date. We can track the examination of public policy implementation literature back to Pressman and Wildavsky's (1973) case study of the difficulties that the city of Oakland, California, encountered when trying to implement a federal manpower training program. The first generation of studies on policy implementation were case studies containing detailed accounts of how a single authoritative decision was carried out (Lester and Lombard, 1987), while the second generation dealt with explaining their success or failure. Lester and Lombard. (1987) offered that a more detailed analysis of these two generations of research may be suggested by four distinct stages during 1970-1987: (1) the generation of case studies; (2) development of policy implementation frameworks; (3) the application of frameworks; and (4) synthesis and revision (p.201).

In the early 1970s, there was very little theoretical research available on the subject of public policy implementation. In spite of the fact that many new public programs were being implemented, there was little knowledge available to assist in the implementation process. As Goggins (1986) notes, initial studies of implementation were detailed accounts of how a single authoritative decision was carried out, either at a single location or at multiple sites. These pioneering works concluded that governmental-sponsored programs seldom achieved their objectives (e.g. Pressman and Wildavsky, 1973). Further, this case study approach made it exceedingly difficult for investigators either to introduce an element of control for extraneous independent variables or to generalize from their findings (Goggins, 1986). It can be argued that early investigators were plagued with problems of too many variables, small sample sizes, or over-determination, where two variables explain equally well the variations in a particular phenomenon.

By the mid 1970s, policy implementation scholars began to turn their attention toward the next stage of intellectual development- model building. Some scholars sought to develop analytical frameworks that were capable of identifying the factors that contribute to the realization (or non-realization) of policy objectives. The work that was conducted in this area can be broadly classified into "top-down" and "bottom-up" approaches (Linder and Peters, 1987). In particular, the top-down approach starts with a policy decision by central government officials and then asks:

1. To what extent were the actions of implementing officials and target groups congruent with (the objectives and procedures) outlined in that policy decision?

2. To what extent what the objectives attained over time, i.e. to what extent were the impacts consistent with the objectives?

3. What were the principal factors affecting policy outputs and impacts, both relevant to the official policy and related factors of political significance?

4. How was the policy reformulated over time on the basis of experience? (Lester and Lombard, 1987, p. 201)

The first top-down analysis was undertaken by Donald Van Meter and Carl Van Horn (1975). Their model posited six variables that they believed to shape the linkage between policy and performance. These variables are: (1) policy standards and objectives; (2) policy resources (i.e., funds or other incentives); (3) interorganizational communication and enforcement activities; (4) characteristics of implementing agencies (e.g., staff size, degree of hierarchical control, organizational vitality, etc.); (5) economic, social, and political conditions (e.g., economic resources within the implementing jurisdiction, nature of public opinion, nature of interest group support, etc.); and (6) disposition of the implementation (Van Meter & Van Horn, 1975, pp 462-474).

Other top-down models include those developed by Sabatier and Mazmanian (1980) and Edwards (1980). The most comprehensive list of factors influencing implementation can be found in the work of Sabatier and Mazmanian (1980). They identify seventeen independent variables within three major categories that they believe affect policy implementation. These categories are (1) the tractability of the problem; (2) the ability of statutes to structure implementation; and (3) non-statutory variables affecting implementation. They describe implementation as coming from the center to the periphery and the target group. The center, consisting of the high level officials, is concerned with the attainment of objectives and the reasons they cannot be successfully completed (Holt, 1993).

Using the term "top-down" implies that the top, usually Congress and the federal agencies, is the major decision maker, with all the other parts of the system lumped together as the "down" portion, even though this may include dozens of agencies, scores of subdivisions and hundreds of participants (Holt, 1993).

Another top-down model was developed by George C. Edwards (1980) who identifies four factors that affect implementation: (1) communications; (2) resources; (3) dispositions of implementers; and (4) bureaucratic structure. Thus, the number of variables thought to affect implementation ranged from four (Edwards, 1980) to seventeen (Sabatier and Mazmanian, 1980).

In contrast to the top-down approach, the bottom-up approach starts by identifying the network of actors involved in service delivery in one or more local areas and asks them about their goals, strategies, activities, and contacts (Lester et al., 1987). "It then uses the contacts as a means for developing a network technique to identify the local, regional, and national actors involved in the planning, financing, and execution of the relevant governmental and non-governmental programs" (Sabatier, 1986, p. 32). Holt (1993) points out that the vocabulary of a top-down approach includes the terms "central control", "coordination", "speed" and "consistency"; the bottom-up approach uses phases such as "local adaptation", "broad participation" and "diversity". Lester et al. (1987) argue that rather than control by central decision-makers, policy is determined by bargaining, either explicit or implicit, between members of the organization and their clients. Therefore, "programs must be compatible with the wishes and desires, or at least the behavioral patterns, of those lower echelon officials" (Linder and Peters, 1987). As a result, this approach received a great deal of criticism for assuming that policy implementation occurs (or could occur) in a decentralized policy making environment (Linder and Peters, 1987). Thus, the bottom-up approach errs in accepting an empirical difficulty as both a normative statement and the sole basis of analysis of a complex organizational and political problem (Linder and Peters, 1987).

Various scholars have been involved in efforts to test these top-down and bottom-up models of policy implementation and have come up with at least three attempts to incorporate the best features of each of the two approaches. Richard Elmore (1985) developed the first approach (in the United States) by combining his earlier work on backward mapping with a new approach that dubbed "forward mapping". In this initial synthesis, he argues that policy makers need to consider both the policy instruments and other resources at their disposal (forward mapping) together with the incentive structure of ultimate target groups (backward mapping), because program success is contingent on combining both of these two considerations.

Another approach was developed by Paul Sabatier(1986), who combined the bottom-uppers' unit of analysis (i.e., a whole variety of public and private actors involved with a policy problem) with the top-downers' concerns over the manner in which socioeconomic conditions and legal instruments constrain behavior. Sabatier's model of policy implementation is primarily concerned with theory construction rather than providing guidelines for practitioners or detailed portraits of particular situations. His model focuses on policy change (i.e. policy formation, policy implementation, and policy reformulation).

The third attempt to synthesize elements of both the top-down and bottom-up approaches was developed by Goggins et al. (1990). In this model of intergovernmental policy implementation, they argue that state implementation is in turn a function of inducements and constraints provided to, or imposed upon, the states from elsewhere in the federal system - above or below - as well as of the states' own propensities to act and their capacity to effectuate their preferences. It should be noted that state choices are not those of a unitary rational actor, but may be the result of bargaining among parties internal or external to government who are involved in state politics (Goggins et al., 1990). Thus, this approach assumes that state implementation of federal programs is ultimately dependent upon both top-down and bottom-up types of variables (Lester and Lombard, 1987).

A number of scholars have offered critical reflection on the status of implementation research. Lester and Lombard, (1987), observe three major areas of concern: (1) theoretical pluralism in implementation research; (2) the restricted nature of implementation research; and (3) the non-cumulative nature of implementation research. After more than twenty years of implementation research, there still is not an overarching implementation perspective that adequately explains and predicts how and why the joint efforts of the American states turn out the way they do. Essentially, there is no theory of implementation that commands general agreement; researchers continue to work from diverse theoretical perspectives, employing different variables to make sense of their findings (O'Toole and Montjoy, 1984). Nevertheless, Lester and Lombard (1987), argue that the available literature does seek to identify the common causes and cures for policy failures. In examining over 100 studies of implementation research, O'Toole found that "most of the pieces referenced …merely identify important variables presented as a checklist or in a theoretically-oriented discussion of the implementation process, without specifying a fully-developed model of implementation" (1986, p. 184). Goggins (1986), argue that what is needed is to identify the "crucial variables" affecting policy implementation. By this they mean that research must be concerned with reducing the number of variables to those few that are "critical". This opinion is diametrically opposed to the approach taken by Mazmanian and Sabatier (1983), who produced the most comprehensive treatment of the factors that influence public policy implementation. What is wrong with their approach? According to Ingram (1980), in their quest to include every factor, the list Mazmanian and Sabatier provide loses focus and becomes too cumbersome to use as a framework for analysis.

Another set of criticisms focuses on the severely restricted context under which implementation research has been conducted. Lester et. al (1987) argue that implementation research has been too restricted in time (emphasizing cross-sectional over longitudinal analysis), number (emphasizing the case study over comparative analysis), policy type investigated (emphasizing a single policy type over multiple policy types), definition of the concept of implementation (focusing on a single output measure rather than multiple measures), and approach (utilizing either the "top-down" or "bottom-up" approach but not both). Yet another, criticism of implementation research is that there are a wide variety of approaches to implementation, but little attempt to build on the works of others. Palumbo and Calista (1990) argue that scholars look upon themselves as idea entrepreneurs, each trying to build his or her own intellectual identification instead of building on the work of others. As a result, the literature goes in all directions.

The final criticism of policy implementation research is that there has been little theoretical synthesis of the extant research (O'Toole, 1986). In short, although "implementation researchers were extremely busy, their results did not seem commensurate with their profligate activities" (Wittrock and DeLeon, 1986, p. 46). Virtually all scholars of policy implementation agree that the next phase of research must be directed toward theory development (Lester and Lombard, 1987). They argue that the next set of questions to be addressed should be designed to illuminate what we know so little about, namely, the full range of outcomes that lie between the extremes of implementation success and failure, the various causal paths leading to each type of outcome, the frequency with which they occur, and their relative importance in implementation outcomes.

The planning and implementation literature are relevant to this study. The planning approach used by NPR is the rational comprehensive planning model. Of all the planning models, the best known, according to Kaiser (1985), and most wisely used for long range planning is rational planning with its systematic forward progression from goal setting to implementation and back again through a feedback loop. Further, Carlson and Awkerman (1991) include setting goals, determining objectives, making plans, implementing the plans, and reviewing the results. To this end, it is virtually impossible to probe the SSA process without having a basic understanding of the planning theories or models. Planning, in this case, is critical to the understanding of variable selection and how they are related to the project concepts and objectives and how these concepts and objectives are not to be applied to achieve the project mission.

The implementation literature is relevant because this is a study of the implementation of NPR. NPR was created from above (the executive branch) following a top down approach. The top-down approach to implementation, according to Holt (1993), points out the vocabulary in this approach which includes central control, coordination, speed, and consistency. The central question investigated in this research is how well the NPR process worked- how field administrators perceived the process, and whether their views mirrors the image of the process envisioned by its creators.

Conclusion

This chapter examined what previous scholars have explored in understanding organizational change, leadership, organizational culture. All these are only part of the important pieces in uncovering whether NPR did create organizational change within SSA. This chapter focused on reviewing the state of knowledge as revealed by the literature concerning some essential areas that are central to this research. The topics discussed included an understanding of the development of an organization's life cycle, the internal organizational dynamic of organizational change, inner leadership, and organizational culture. NPR is central a question of policy implementation and will be examined as such. All these components are important when reviewing the complex topic of organizational change. The next chapter discusses the historical development of the SSA, and provides insight into the problems and responsibilities of this public institution.

Chapter 3 The Social Security Administration (SSA)

We can never insure one hundred percent of the population against one hundred percent of the hazards and vicissitudes of life, but we have tried to frame a law which will give some measure of protection to the average citizen and to his family against the loss of a job and against poverty-ridden old age.

This law, too, represents a cornerstone in a structure which is being built but is by no means complete. It is a structure intended to lessen the force of possible future depressions. It will act as a protection to future Administrations against the necessity of going deeply into debt to furnish relief to the needy. The law will flatten out the peaks and valleys of deflation and of inflation. It is, in short, a law that will take care of human needs and at the same time provide the United States an economic structure of vastly greater soundness.

President Franklin Roosevelt
August 14, 1935- Remarks at signing of the Social Security Act

The Social Security Act of 1935 (49 Stat., 620) was implemented in an attempt to deal with major changes in the nature of the economy, social needs and equity, and attitudes regarding retirement. The program has changed significantly since its inception, and has expanded to include the provision of economic security in the event of retirement, disability, or death of the principal income earner.

The organizational structure of the Social Security Administration (SSA) is vast and complex and has undergone significant institutional changes, especially in the past twenty-five years. It is now an independent agency. The changes were created not only by its environment but also by the changing focus of its leadership, and this chapter explores these areas along with the dynamics of constant organizational change within this mature public institution.

This chapter primarily is a brief overview of SSA. It begins with an explanation of why there is a need for a program like Social Security and the initiation by the federal government of this social insurance program. Traces the legislative history of SSA with a description of the current programs. It concludes with a broad overview of the organizational structure of SSA as well as a discussion of the changes between 1975-2000.

Social Security?

As a result of the worldwide economic changes triggered by the industrial revolution, workers found themselves competing for jobs in manufacturing rather than relying on the family farm. These new jobs tended to be stable, lucrative, and near the big cities. However, the changes in the American economy due to industrialization, urbanization, and specialization created the need to address retirement issues.

Originally the country's economic base was agricultural commerce, but the industrial revolution created a shift toward more dependence on industrial and manufacturing commerce (Tynes, 1996). Working in the factories offered higher wages, stable jobs, and less dependence on the forces of nature. However, the workers were now in an environment that focused on a 40-hour work week and a limited working life. This led to mandatory retirement, as in industrialized economies younger workers are favored over their older counterparts because of their productivity potential (Kingson and Schulz, 1997; Meyers, 1993). Younger workers migrated to the urban centers, while those older Americans left behind were no longer able to depend on their extended families to care for them in their retirement years.

The industrial revolution changed the way that individuals worked by requiring more specialization to increase production, thereby favoring younger workers over older workers and forcing many older workers to retire. Mechanical advances simplified processes and increased production. This reduced the amount of manpower needed, while the scientific management movement attempted to increase productivity and profitability. Focusing on economic security was a response not only to these dramatic shifts in the culture but also to other economic factors.

In 1929, the crash of the stock market caused a ripple effect that closed banks, businesses, and factories across America and pushed the unemployment rate to over 25%, triggering the Great Depression (Americans Discuss Social Security, 1998). This fragile economic environment created a tense political climate. There was an increase in homelessness, especially among older workers and farmers. This created a sense of distress, and angry voters demanding action picketed state capitols. Unlike earlier recessions, this world-wide depression impacted the life of every American. After the prosperous roaring twenties, there was a harsh shift downward in which people lost their jobs, fortunes, homes, and economic stability. The problem was not that workers were lazy, but that there was simply no work for them to do. The pillars of the past were gone, state and local governments were financially strapped, and the financial institutions had simply collapsed.

However, as a community Americans have historically been geared toward helping the less fortunate, believing that when people have no other means of subsistence, they must be supported from public funds (Witte, 1955). Robert Reich described these values as deeply ingrained in the American psyche (Reich, 1987).

A dramatic social change was clearly needed, and Franklin Roosevelt was elected on his promise to take action (Nash, Pugash, and Tomasson, 1988, pp. 38-39). In his campaign, he stressed the need for the federal government to ensure the economic security of its citizens. The significance of this message was that instead of relying on individual responsibility for economic security, the federal government would create programs to support and assist the needs of the citizenry. Roosevelt's advocacy, coupled with the harsh economic times, caused significant numbers of Americans to support the idea of federal government assistance programs, and by electing President Roosevelt the American people clearly showed that they favored government intervention. The changes in society caused by the Great Depression served as a catalyst for the creation of the Social Security program.

Internationally, attitudes regarding economic security had also been changing and many governments were beginning to adopt government-sponsored programs. The term "social security" was originally coined by Simón Bolivar, the South American champion of independence from Spanish colonial rule, who proclaimed, "The system of government most perfect is that which produces the greatest amount of happiness possible, the greatest amount of social security, and the greatest amount of political stability" (Carter and Shipman, 1996, p. 39).

The advent of mandatory retirement and a lack of individual planning for retirement created a need for a government-mandated social insurance program, extending a basic level of income security to workers. The industrial revolution and Great Depression dramatized how American workers had become financially dependent on factors beyond their control, shifting the attitudes of the American public, interest groups, and politicians and leading to their eventual support of government-sponsored retirement programs for all workers.

During the late 1800s, countries all over the world were setting up programs to protect the economic security of older workers and attempted to deal with the effects of the industrial revolution. Eleven countries adopted compulsory unemployment laws between 1919 and 1930 (Kingston and Schultz, 1997). For example, Otto Von Bismark of Germany sponsored a government-funded retirement program for the elderly that provided income support for Germans aged 65 and over, even though the average life expectancy at the time was only 55 (Walker, 1997, p. 17).

In America, there were many advocates of government-sponsored retirement programs. For example, Robert Townsend, a doctor from Long Beach, California, called for a pension of $200 a month for every citizen over 60 who agreed to stop working and spend each month's allotment within 30 days. The scheme was appealing because it would remove millions of people from the crowded labor market and provide a boost to the economy from the new spending (Americans Discuss Social Security, 1998). At its peak over 7,000 Townsend clubs were organized, with over two million members (SSA, 1998a). With such overwhelming support, groups such as Dr. Townsend's significantly influenced the introduction of the social security legislation (Anderson, 1990, p.68; Holtzman, 1965). The stage was set for the creation of some type of social insurance for the American worker.

Formation of the Social Security Program

The Social Security program was an attempt to address the economic challenges facing working Americans. Industrialization, urbanization, and the Great Depression provided a backdrop that highlighted the frailties of the free market and the need for government-sponsored social insurance. The real question facing American's political leaders was: what was going to be done to alleviate the problems affecting the economic welfare of working Americans? Partly as a result of initiatives by political leaders, the American people, and interest groups, the new government-sponsored economic security program was formulated and adopted in a relatively short period of time (Anderson, 2000).

Social Security Act of 1935

The Social Security Act, which was only thirty two pages long, stated in the prologue that its intent was:

To provide for general welfare by establishing a system of Federal old age benefits, and by enabling the several states to make more adequate provision for aged persons, blind persons, dependent and crippled children, maternal and child welfare, public health, and the administration of their unemployment compensation laws; to establish a Social Security Board; to raise revenue; and for other purposes (Nash, Pugash and Tomasson, 1988, p. 8)

The major provisions of the Act were: Title I. Grants to States for Old-Age Assistance, which supported welfare programs for the aged; and Title II. Federal Old-Age Benefits. The latter was the new social insurance program, now known as Social Security. In the Social Security Act of 1935, benefits were to be paid to the primary worker upon reaching the age of 65 and were to be based on payroll tax contributions paid during their working life. These taxes were first to be collected in 1937 and workers would be eligible to begin to receive monthly payments in 1942.

The effective leadership set forth by President Franklin Roosevelt and the Congress coupled with the cooperation of involved groups, the passage of Social Security Act of 1935 was possible. However, even the President acknowledged that the signing of the Social Security Act of 1935 was "a cornerstone in a structure which was being built but was by no means complete" (Driver, 1985, p. 30). The next important step was to institutionalize this legislation into a new federal agency.

Social Security originated as an income replacement system for its beneficiaries, which was initially framed as a retirement system for the elderly. This program was not simply a welfare program, but basic universal social insurance in which benefits were based on the amount invested into the program over a lifetime of work. However, other needs required important consideration, such as the expanding pool of workers to be covered and their need for additional benefits. From the beginning, Social Security was expected to adapt and change with the shifting needs of the American public over time and, as a result, today the Social Security program grants benefits to retirees, the disabled, and survivors. The Social Security program is neither a covenant nor a contract, but an expression of community that reaffirms some of the program's most important traditional values, enhancing the familiar claim that all Americans have a stake in the program and acknowledging that sustaining mutual interdependence in the American community presupposes both a shared past and a common future (Nash, Pugash, and Tomasson, 1988).

The significance of this program is that it sought a long-term solution to economic security for the aged. An individual would pay into a public trust fund and earn credits applicable toward benefits in retirement. This would only be part of an individual's retirement planning and would be supplemented by personal savings and company pension programs. This program was distinct from the welfare benefits paid by the state "old age programs," as the Social Security program was a social insurance program rather than a public welfare program. President Roosevelt conceived Title I as a temporary relief program that would eventually disappear as more individuals were able to obtain retirement income through the contributory system. This system was a moderate approach compared to many of the other proposals put forward at the time (SSA, 1998a).

In 1939, legislation changed the program to include survivor benefits paid to aged widows and parents, and children under age 18. This transformation made Social Security shift from simply being a retirement program toward one focused on family-based economic security. The 1939 amendments also shifted benefits to begin in 1940. By expanding the range of benefits to include survivors' benefits, deciding that married couples should receive higher benefits than single workers, and lowering the size of the reserve fund, Congress helped ease some of the pressure on the program.

On January 31, 1940, Ida M. Fuller became the first person to receive an old age monthly benefit check under the Social Security law. She had paid $49.68 a year between 1937 and 1939 on her income of $2,484 and her first Social Security check was for $22.54. She continued to collect payments until her death in 1975 at 100 years of age, having received a total of $22,888.92 in Social Security benefits (SSA, 2000a).

With the amendments to the Social Security Act expanding its administrative authority, the agency changed in management style. Organizationally, for the first year or two (1936-1937), overall management functions (personnel, budget, etc.) were handled by the Accounts and Audits and Business Management Offices for all the Social Security Board. Also during this period, the various Operating and Servicing Bureaus and Offices were established rudimentary parallel management functions of their own. On July 1, 1939, the Social Security Board lost its independent agency status when the new cabinet-level Federal

Security Agency was created. The Federal Security Agency was composed of the Social Security Board, the Public Health Service, the Office of Education, the Civilian Conservation Corps, and the U.S. Employment Service. From 1939-1953, the Social Security Board, later known as the SSA, was under the jurisdiction of the Federal Security Agency.

The controversy with Social Security was due to the fact that for individual workers more benefits were received from state programs than from Social Security. These inequities lead to an advisory council being established to look into these programs in 1947 and 1948. On August 28, 1950, after considerable scrutiny and debate, the recommendations of the advisory council became law. Through this law, the proponents of Social Security gained much of what they wanted, in particular a greatly expanded Social Security program that paid substantially higher benefits. An increasing tax rate was established to reach a maximum of 6.5 percent by 1970. Another important feature was that self-employed persons could pay Social Security taxes through their income taxes. Arthur Altmeyer, who was in charge of the program during the Roosevelt and Truman years, describes these changes as crucial to the survival of the program. It meant that Social Security had finally attained parity with welfare (Achenbaum, 1986; Altmeyer, 1966, p. 169).

The Social Security Amendments of 1954 provided additional coverage against economic insecurity by initiating the disability insurance program. The program was initially set to freeze workers' Social Security records during the years they were unable to work, preventing survivor and retirement benefits from being reduced. In 1956, the program was amended to give benefits to disabled workers aged 50-65, disabled adults and children. Congress then took steps to further broaden the coverage over the next two years, permitting disabled workers under age 50 and their dependents to qualify for benefits (SSA, 1998a). The disability programs are funded by the Social Security Trust Fund and are paid to beneficiaries who can show that they are disabled. This addition to the Social Security program was another step toward the overall economic security of the worker. In the 1950's, the coverage extended to all industrial workers and the armed forces, and was on a voluntary basis for the self-employed, however, it was still optional for state and local governments.

1965 Medicare benefits

For years concern was developed about the inadequate health coverage for American's seniors. President Truman was the first to advocate the formation of some form of universal health care for the elderly. Unfortunately Congress was deadlocked and nothing was accomplished because the concern was over the beginning of socialized health care. This changed when President Johnson took on this controversial cause and was able to steward the legislation using his political clout and aggressive tactics (Berkowitz, 1995). President Johnson signed the Medicare bill on July 30, 1965 at the Truman Library in Missouri, paying tribute to former President Truman. Johnson even signed up President Truman as the first Medicare recipient. Social Security became responsible for administering a new social insurance program that extended health coverage to almost all Americans aged 65 or older (SSA, 1998a). The addition of Medicare resulted in a major reorganization of SSA that lasted for almost ten years. This new program dramatically expanded the responsibilities of SSA and increased the recruitment and growth of the bureaucracy.

Although this program is administered by the SSA, its revenues come from the Medicare tax. The program provides partial medical coverage for the elderly and was advanced by Lyndon Johnson as a response to the lack of adequate medical benefits for the elderly as part of his "Great Society" initiative designed to establish programs that would expand the reaches of government.

Another change to the program's benefits occurred with the 1972 cost of living allowances (COLAs). Prior to the 1972 amendments, which introduced cost of living allowances and other automatic provisions, several assumptions had been made and long range cost estimates included as a safety factor (Ball, 1998, p. 34). The 1972 legislation set an annual automatic cost of living allowance, beginning in 1975, based on the annual increase in consumer prices. This by passed the need to have special legislation by Congress to increase benefits and prevent inflation from reducing the benefits. One important result insured that beneficiaries would continue to keep up with the rising cost of living and also prevent future increases from becoming politicized.

In the early 1970s, for the first time of the history of the program, the seventy-five year projections showed a shortfall for the program, as the projected revenues were insufficient to sustain the amount of benefits paid out. After the 1972 amendments were enacted, the program was expected to be solvent for 75 years. Due to the oil crisis and changes in economic assumptions, more changes had to be made in 1977, in which the program was said to be in balance for another 50 years. Unfortunately, higher inflation and a second oil crisis in 1979 again undermined the financing plans.

In the 1970s, the agency's responsibilities expanded with the introduction of a new program, Supplemental Security Income (SSI). In order to qualify for this program, an economic need was required. Previously, the state and local governments had been administering "adult categories" programs with partial federal funding for the needy aged, blind, and disabled. Over time, state administered programs had become complicated and inconsistent, with as many as 1,350 different agencies involved. President Nixon identified a need to "bring reason, order, and purpose into a tangle of overlapping programs." In 1971, Secretary of Health, Education, and Welfare, Elliott Richardson, proposed that SSA assume responsibility for these "adult categories." This would assure those benefits be the same nationally. The 1972 amendments to the Social Security Act assigned the administration of the Supplementary Security Income program to SSA. However, the funding did not come from the FICA tax but general government revenues (SSA, 1998a).

The SSA is an independent agency within the executive branch of the government. The agency is responsible for administering Social Security programs throughout the United States, paying out benefits to over 43 million people and providing protection to more than 141 million workers. The Commissioner of Social Security is nominated by the president and confirmed by the Senate, and serves for a term of seven years which may be renewed, or a new commissioner is brought in. However, as a part of the President's cabinet, the commissioner serves at the pleasure of the President and may be removed at any time.

The agency has approximately 65,000 employees, with the central staff located primarily in Baltimore, Maryland. It provides direct service to the public through over a thousand facilities managed regionally by ten civil service public administrators. These individual regions focus on the objective of effectively administering the Social Security program. /figure 1/

These SSA facilities include 1,343 Social Security field offices, 36 tele-service centers, one data operations center, and seven processing centers located throughout the United States and its territories. They also include program service centers in six major U.S. cities, which service the records of most beneficiaries and provide back up answering capability for the 800 number telephone service. Direct service to the public is also provided by the Office of Disability and International Operations and the Office of Central Records Operations in Baltimore and Wilkes-Barre, Pennsylvania, respectively. The Office of Hearings of Appeals administers the nationwide hearings and appeals program for the SSA at 133 sites. In addition, the states operate 54 Disability Determination Services agencies nationwide. Their operations, conducted by approximately 14,000 state employees, are fully funded through the SSA (SSA, 1998e).

Figure 3 1 Social Security Administration (SSA) Regional Boundaries

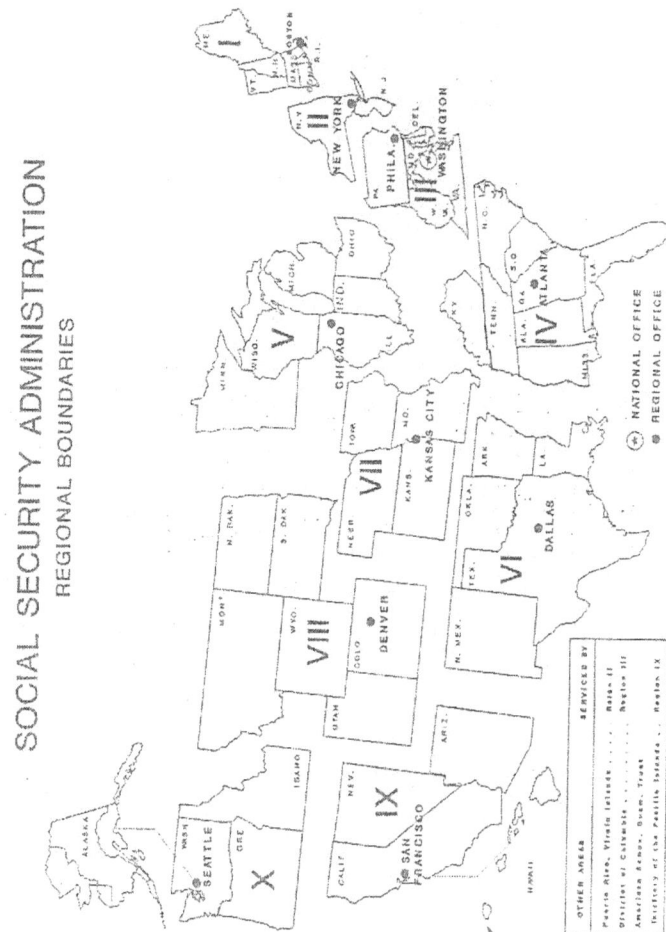

The Southern Region of the Social Security Administration (SSA)

The specific focus of this research is on the Southern Region of the SSA which covers the eight

southern states: North Carolina, South Carolina, Kentucky, Tennessee, Georgia, Florida, Alabama, and

Mississippi. The region serves over 9 million Social Security beneficiaries who receive over $6 billion each

month. The Southern regional offices are in Atlanta, Georgia. The organizational structure is highly

bureaucratic with many overlying layers, and policy guidance is provided by the national headquarters.

The linkage from the national offices to the field offices operates as follows: the President appoints

the Commissioner, who has a staff of deputies. The Deputy Commissioner for Operations oversees the

regional commissioner. The regional commissioner has a staff that includes individual state directors from

each of the southern states, who in turn oversee the local district offices where the claimants go to file claims as seen in figures 3.2, 3.3, and 3.4. There are 254 Social Security offices throughout the Atlanta Region who provide in-person or telephone service to local clients. In addition, four of the national telephone service sites, which are located in this region, handle over 40 million calls a year. The region also has 31 Offices of Hearings and Appeals (OHA) to handle reconsideration and appeal cases, nine federally funded state Disability Determination Service (DDS) units, and a large Program Service Center (PSC).

47

Figure 3 2 Social Security Administration (SSA) Organizational Chart

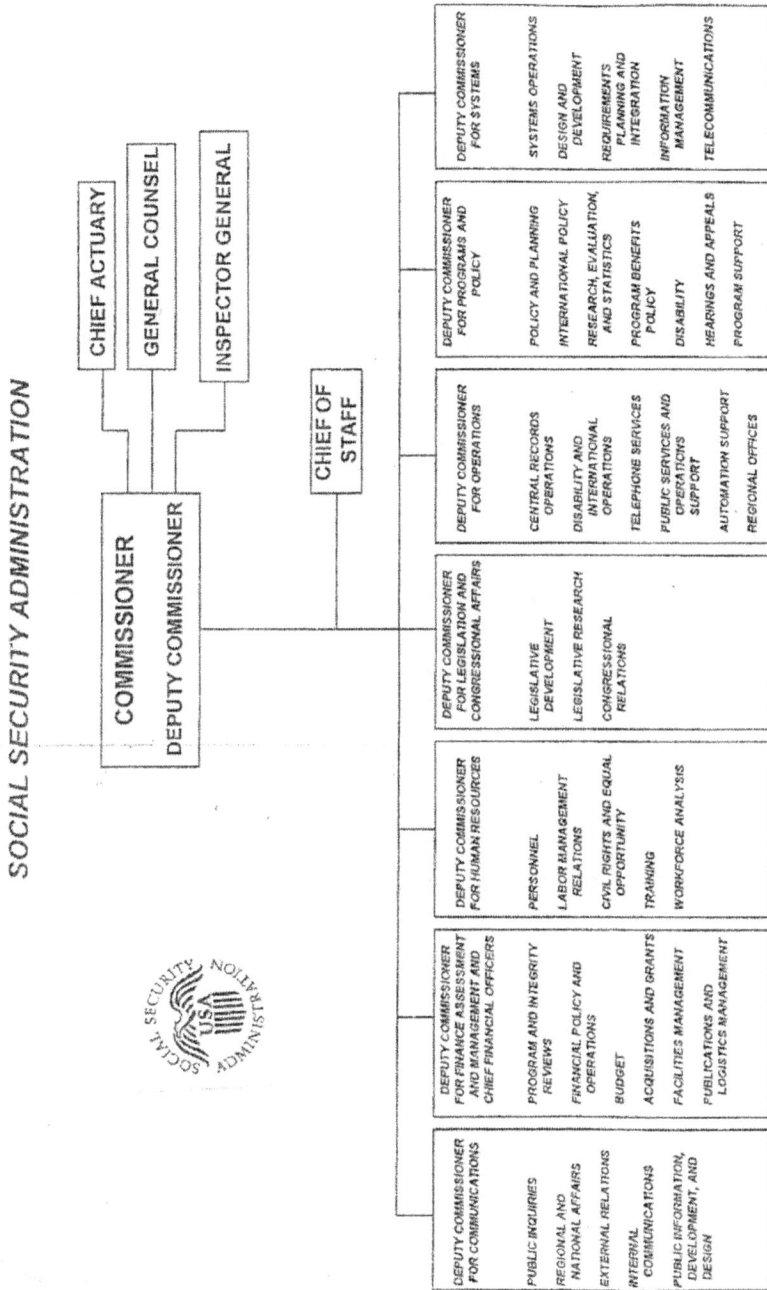

Figure 3 3 Social Security Administration (SSA) Atlanta Regional Office Chart

OFFICE OF THE REGIONAL COMMISSIONER
ATLANTA REGION

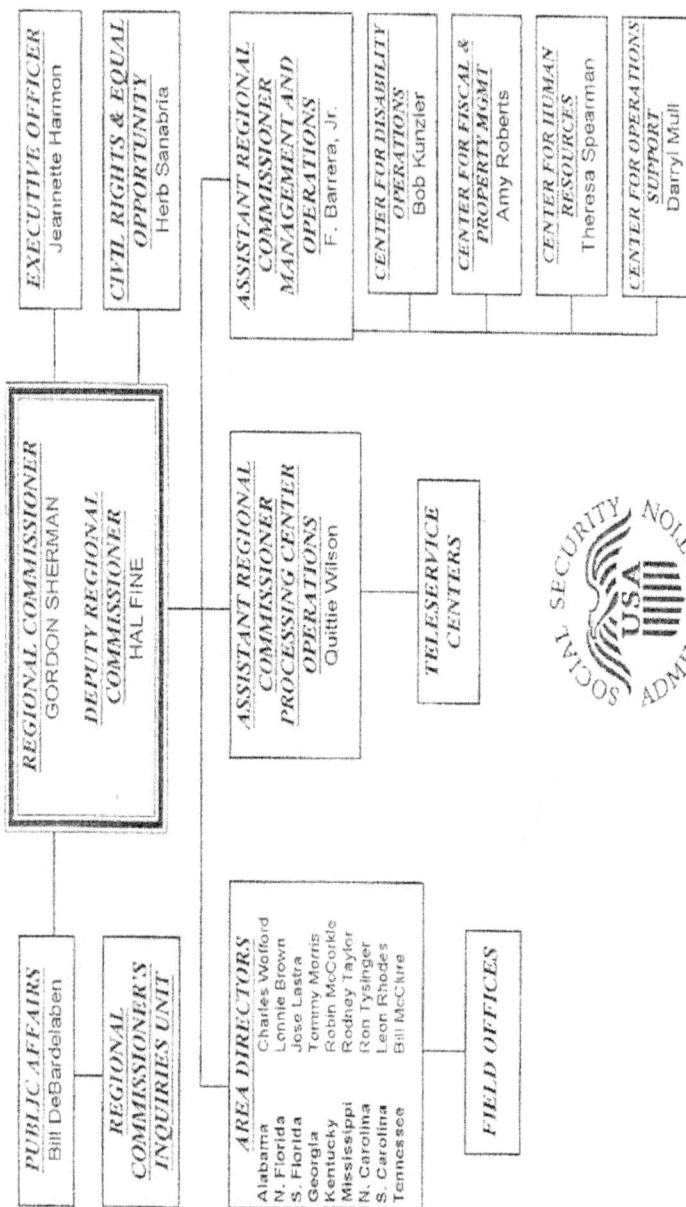

REGIONAL COMMISSIONER
GORDON SHERMAN

DEPUTY REGIONAL COMMISSIONER
HAL FINE

EXECUTIVE OFFICER
Jeannette Harmon

CIVIL RIGHTS & EQUAL OPPORTUNITY
Herb Sanabria

ASSISTANT REGIONAL COMMISSIONER MANAGEMENT AND OPERATIONS
F. Barrera, Jr.

CENTER FOR DISABILITY OPERATIONS
Bob Kunzler

CENTER FOR FISCAL & PROPERTY MGMT
Amy Roberts

CENTER FOR HUMAN RESOURCES
Theresa Spearman

CENTER FOR OPERATIONS SUPPORT
Darryl Mull

ASSISTANT REGIONAL COMMISSIONER PROCESSING CENTER OPERATIONS
Quittie Wilson

TELESERVICE CENTERS

PUBLIC AFFAIRS
Bill DeBardelaben

REGIONAL COMMISSIONER'S INQUIRIES UNIT

AREA DIRECTORS

Alabama	Charles Wofford
N. Florida	Lonnie Brown
S. Florida	Jose Lastra
Georgia	Tommy Morris
Kentucky	Robin McCorkle
Mississippi	Rodney Taylor
N. Carolina	Ron Tysinger
S. Carolina	Leon Rhodes
Tennessee	Bill McClure

FIELD OFFICES

Figure 3 4 Social Security Administration Field Facilities and Staff

ATLANTA REGION
SSA FIELD FACILITIES AND STAFF

106	LEVEL ONE OFFICES
95	LEVEL TWO OFFICES
52	LEVEL THREE OFFICES
1	LEVEL FOUR OFFICE
2	TELESERVICE CENTERS
1	MEGA TELESERVICE CENTER
360	CONTACT STATIONS
1	PROGRAM SERVICE CENTER
9	STATE DIRECTOR OFFICES
31	HEARINGS & APPEALS OFFICES
10	RESIDENT STATIONS
9	STATE DISABILITY DETERMINATION SECTIONS (19 DDS UNITS)
1	REGIONAL PROGRAM AND INTEGRITY REVIEWS

SSA EMPLOYEE TOTAL   9,787*
STATE DDS EMPLOYESS   3,005*

*INCLUDES SEPSC, TSC, RO, OHA, RPIR, AND FIELD EMPLOYEES

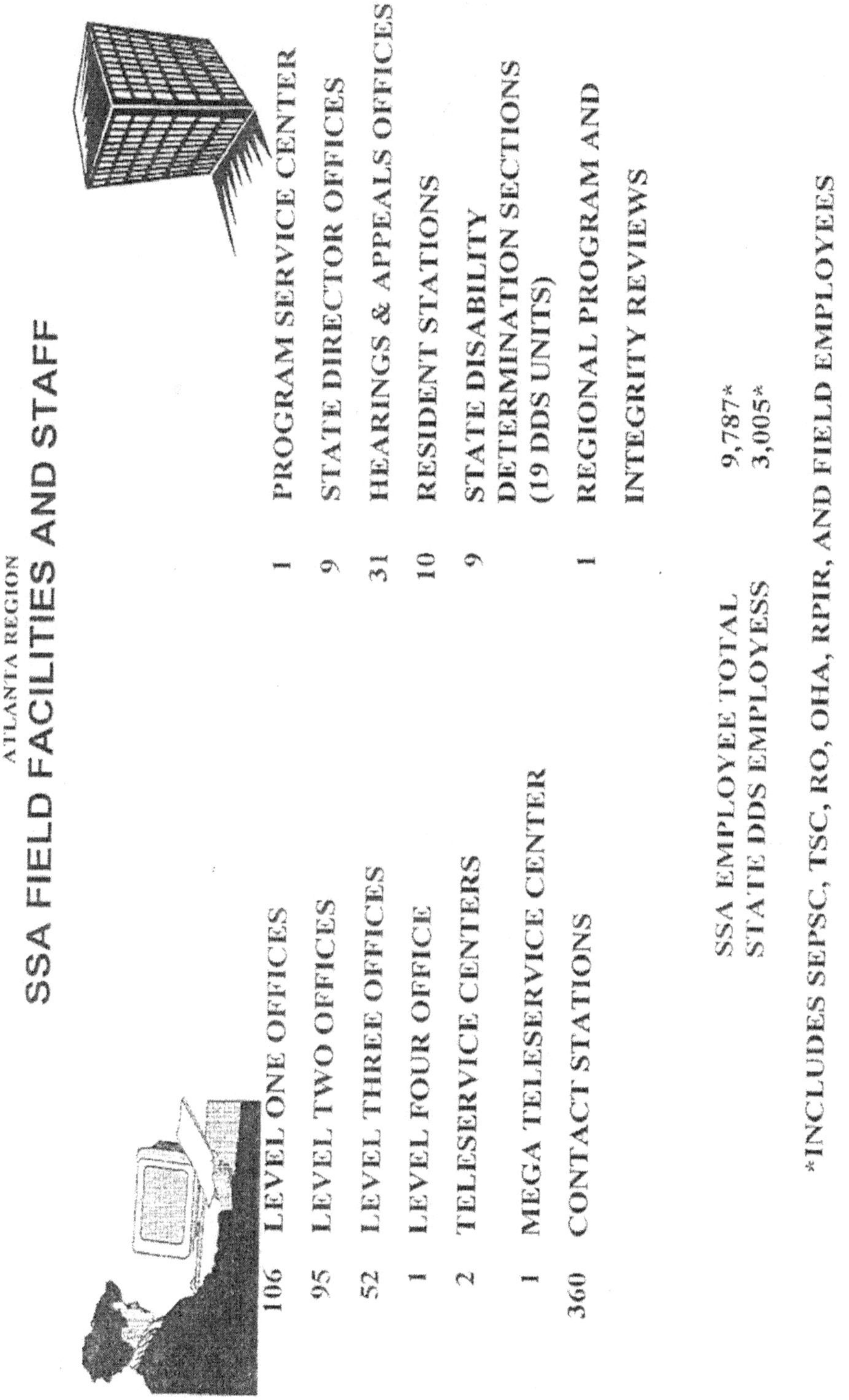

Policy Development

The mission of the SSA is: "To administer national Social Security programs as prescribed by legislation, in an equitable, efficient, and caring manner" (SSA, 2000b). The strategic planning process in the SSA has allowed the agency to deal with the issues created by increasing workloads, decreasing resources, and changing technological innovations in accomplishing its mission (SSA, 1996). Strategic management includes planning, budgeting, implementing, tracking, and monitoring the agency's performance in both the administrative and policy making arenas.

The agency administers the Social Security program which includes two areas: the Old Age, Survivors' and Disability Insurance; and Supplementary Security Income. To do this effectively, the agency issues Social Security numbers to eligible individuals; maintains lifelong earnings records for individuals working under employment covered by Social Security; takes claim for benefits; adjudicates appeals on disputed decisions; and processes millions of transactions annually to keep the beneficiary records current. The SSA also administers aspects of the Medicare, Medicaid, and Black Lung and Coal Industry Retirement Health Benefit program and serves a key role in ensuring the integrity of other federally-funded needs-based benefit programs.

The agency's activities are focused, but not limited to, a few key areas. Other areas of activity include enumeration, earnings, claims, post entitlement, informing the public and service delivery interface. The legislative authority of SSA determines the standards of eligibility, levels of benefits, and the amount of additional earnings permitted, and other consideration for old age and survivor's benefits. (Anderson, 1990, p. 174) The organizational culture of the agency as a whole is a complex mixture of national and regional differences. The Southern Region possesses its own unique character, due to a combination of individual state cultural differences and the high concentration of retirees living in Florida.

Organizational Changes in a Maturing Public Agency 1975-2000

Between 1975 and 2000, the SSA focused on three major areas of development: (a) legislative changes, (b) implementation of strategic planning, and (c) administrative and political leadership changes.

The SSA was also faced with decreasing operational budgets and a push for more efficiency. As a result, the agency increasingly began to make use of strategic management to help deal with these problems without adversely affecting clients. In addition to the planning and budgeting activities, strategic management focused on strategic thinking: seeing the strategic value of work done, recognizing when no strategic value exists, identifying new work that provides strategic value, and making the strategic choices that will move the agency forward. At the same time, Congress passed legislation that mandated performance measures.

Political and administrative leadership led to changes in the priorities within the agency. The massive expansion that took place during the early years of the program slowed down, and fewer employees were recruited to deal with the increasing workloads. Social Security became a politically sensitive program, whose clients were important political constituencies for elected officials. Thus, few major legislative changes could be passed. Legislation concerning Old Age, Survivors and Dependents Insurance focused on three fundamental areas: maintaining the value of benefits over time; assuring the financial soundness of the system; and structuring the disability program so as to maintain its responsiveness to the needs of the disabled while curbing the potential for abuse.

The earliest document that could be considered a strategic plan is the *Master Plan for the Development of the Future Social Security Process*, published in 1975. The *Master Plan* was produced in response to a letter from President Ford addressing the need for an overall strategic plan after the Supplemental Security Income program was enacted and Social Security was given the task of administering the program, in 1974. The transfer of additional responsibilities led to a mass hiring of employees and highlighted the crucial role that automated systems would play. The *Master Plan* foresaw the agency moving toward a paperless process in all areas, thus reducing the need to hire new people, and the possibilities inherent in the implementation of new, more efficient, technology.

In 1979, Stanford Ross was sworn in as Commissioner of SSA and under his leadership the agency undertook a major reorganization. Because of the complexity and substantive nature of the changes, they were gradually phased in over the course of a year. In 1980, the Department of Health and Human Services replaced the Department of Health, Education, and Welfare, of which Social Security was a major part. At the same time, a 1980 amendment to the Social Security Act required the SSA to conduct periodic reviews of current disability beneficiaries to certify their continuing eligibility. This additional workload was controversial, and in 1983 was halted. In 1984, Congress passed the Disability Benefits Reform Act modifying several aspects of the disability program (SSA, 1998a).

The long term financing of Social Security again became a major concern in the 1980's, and President Reagan appointed a bipartisan commission, headed by Alan Greenspan, to look into it. The final bill, signed into law in 1983, made several changes in the program, including the taxation of Social Security benefits, the coverage of Federal employees for the first time, and the raising of the retirement age (Neustadt and May, 1986).

In addition to the problems with the retirement program, the agency also had significant congressionally mandated-program and policy changes imposed in 1981 and 1983. This was compounded by its lack of access to federal administrative dollars, beginning in 1985, and a downsizing that eliminated the jobs of slightly over 17,000 SSA employees through 1990. The agency has been placed under severe stress due to its lack of consistent leadership, had nine commissioners or acting commissioners from 1981-2000 and numerous reorganizations and changes in responsibility for both program administration and policy development. The vulnerability of Social Security funds to deficit reduction efforts continues to jeopardize the agency's ability to run the program efficiently and effectively. The continuous changes severely impact the managers who are responsible for day to day operations, and the increasing workload and decreasing number of full time employees further burden the agency's staff. The result is a SSA that provides a substandard service to its beneficiaries and applicants.

Administrators within the SSA foresaw advances in technology as an important part of administering the program in the future. The *System Modernization Plan* was produced in 1982 and created a new system organization, addressing every area of systems management, from computer operations to software engineering and data communications. It implemented some important management instruments, such as the concept of a rolling plan and a continuous planning mechanism for software development and hardware capacity. Integration of projects and obtaining user input was emphasized. The plan was updated yearly in a special edition directed to users in the field offices.

The limitations of this plan were that the software development schedules were overly ambitious. The plan was created as a direct response to the crisis within the operational systems and focused on systems development rather than an overall business plan. A 1987 General Accounting Office study criticized the plan, saying its focus was on how best to provide automated support for conducting present day workload rather than how to improve overall performance (GAO, 1997a).

The 1987 General Accounting Office study recommended that "Social Security develop an agency-wide long-range plan and revise its systems modernization strategy to be consistent with it" (GAO, 1987). Commissioner Dorcas Hardy responded to the study by directing the agency to prepare the coherent, long-range strategic plan which came to be known as *Social Security 2000- A Strategic Plan*. This plan included a mission statement, "to administer equitably, effectively and efficiently a national program of social insurance as prescribed by legislation" (SSA, 1988, p.1) and created a profile of what the future environment would look like by researching the changing economy, demographics, socioeconomic conditions, and technology. This plan was an aggressive approach by the agency and took a detailed, comprehensive, business-wide look at the future of the organization.

The strategic plan was based on a firm commitment to both the current beneficiaries and to those who work for the SSA. Six operating priorities defined the scope of the plan:

1.   To maintain the fiscal integrity of the Social Security Trust Fund;

2.   To improve public confidence in Social Security and how its programs are operated;

3.   To provide the best possible service for the SSA's customers;

4.   To improve management to facilitate greater effectiveness, efficiency, and accountability;

5.   To use the best and most appropriate technology available to administer SSA programs; and

6.   To continue to ensure that the SSA can count on a properly skilled workforce (SSA 1988, p. 1).

This broad outline was followed with 29 recommendations: three suggestions for program simplification, nine initiatives for improving services, ten enhancements to the way technology was used, and seven proposals in the areas of organization and human resources. These recommendations built on the core of the SSA strategic plan.

As with earlier plans, it contained weaknesses. The technology was not yet sufficiently advanced to meet some of the expectations, many of the program changes required congressional action, most of the projects emphasized detracted from infrastructure-related activities, and the more structured implementation processes discussed in the document never fully materialized. Although the plan drove action, the action was isolated and project specific; its ultimate vision languished while a handful of special projects, whose overall value to the agency might not have justified their high priorities, garnered most of the attention.

Some of the changes proposed by the plan also were viewed as counter to the agency's culture and mission. For example, the establishment of the 800 telephone service was seen as a move away from the more personal service provided by field offices, as was the direct deposit of benefit payments, which was seen both inside and outside the agency as a way to improve efficiency at the expense of the desires of the beneficiaries. Even the references to the beneficiaries as "customers" conjured up images of the business world rather than the public service focus on helping society.

In 1989, Commissioner Gwendolyn King initiated a new plan that would build upon the goals and objectives she had established for the agency. An environmental scan was conducted to identify particular trends applicable to Social Security. The mission statement was modified to "administer national Social Security programs as prescribed by legislation in an equitable, effective, efficient and caring manner" (SSA, 1991, p. 9). Three broad goals defined how the agency was expected to accomplish this mission:

1. To serve the public with compassion, courtesy, consideration, efficiency, and accuracy;

2. To protect and maintain the American people's investment in the Social Security Trust Fund and to instill public confidence in Social Security programs; and

3. To create an environment that ensures a highly skilled workforce dedicated to meeting the challenge of the SSA's public service mission (SSA, 1991, p. 9)

What distinguished this from earlier plans was that future constraints were addressed and five priority areas were used as the foundation of all implementation planning for the next several years. Perhaps the most important feature of the plan was that it created a central element of a unified planning system that included both the agency strategic planning process and the tactical level planning and budgeting system that would support its implementation. Building on the experience of *Social Security 2000*, planners now understood the importance of driving plan execution down to the level of the individual worker in the agency to help ensure that the plan's objectives would permeate daily operations.

The Planning and Budgeting System was implemented before this framework plan was completed. Social Security always has had an annual budget process, and decisions around key agency initiatives were largely driven by the process of building the yearly budget and recommending an appropriate budget to the Commissioner and, ultimately, to Congress. In the 1990 fiscal year, an interim process for proposing and selecting key change initiatives was put in place. Each proposal provided the information necessary to make preliminary decisions about the value of the initiative, including such information as the objective to be achieved, the approach to be used, the schedule for achieving the objective, and an analysis of the costs, benefits, and impact. After the proposals were analyzed by a high level group of component planning representatives, the Commissioner used the report as a basis for deciding which initiatives should be supported in the budget submission. The plan then was translated into tactical plans for the next seven year period, giving executives enough information to make decisions, supporting development of the budget, and guiding the construction of lower level projects.

Executives met throughout the year, in their role as managers of specific activities, to report on initiatives that the SSA was pursuing. They also made decisions about which plans should be eliminated and which revised, and identified areas of emphasis where they would like to see new plans proposed. Detailed instructions were issued, providing the planning schedule for the year. This plan became the framework for constructing the budget, enabling the agency to receive higher appropriations. (Eisenger, 1992).

The plans that followed these early attempts at strategic planning were drastically different. Many factors have led the SSA down a more complex path, but the two most important among them were the influence of the Government Performance Results Act of 1993 along with other statutory changes and

Commissioner Shirley Chater's strong support of the concept of strategic decision making. Chater's concept of strategic planning was that strategic does not mean only "long-range," and that good strategic direction can result from any agency interaction, not just from formal executive activity focused on providing it. The agency facilitators report directly to the Commissioner, and the Office of Strategic Management is directed by a member of the executive staff and staffed by people whose responsibilities include integrating information resources, management policy, and facilitating process improvement at the SSA, as well as managing the unified planning system and addressing other agency-wide issues.

During this period, the new Clinton administration implemented a program focused on "reinventing government" by creating the National Performance Review (NPR). Vice-President Al Gore was appointed to lead this program aimed at examining current government practices and making recommendations on ways to make government "work better and cost less." The development of the NPR is examined in the next chapter.

A major obstacle facing the agency dealt with the problem of the adjudication of disability claims within the disability program. Commissioner Chater wanted to redesign the procedures in the disability program, and began a major redesign of the way in which the program was administered. The case for action was presented effectively, and in September 1994 she announced plans to pursue aggressively the reengineering of the disability program (Chater, 1997).

The passage of the Government Performance Results Act (GPRA) of 1993 by Congress required every government agency to submit a strategic plan that would contain several important components: a comprehensive mission statement, a list of general goals, and a list of objectives. The plan would also include a description of how the general goals and objectives were to be achieved and the relationship between the performance goals in the annual performance plan and the general goals and objectives in the strategic plan. The plan would identify those key factors external to the agency and beyond its control that could affect significantly whether or not it achieved its objective and describe the type of program evaluation used, along with a schedule for future program evaluations. Each strategic plan spans a minimum six-year period: the fiscal year in which it is submitted and at least five fiscal years forward from that date, and must be revised and updated at least once every three years (GAO, 1997b).

The operational budget for the SSA has shifted since its inception, and is now appropriated by Congress, even though the funds actually come from the Social Security Trust Fund. As a result of the adoption of the GPRA, the agency has to justify its budget by using performance measures. In the 1980s and 1990s, there was growing bipartisan support for removing Social Security from the Health and Human Services cabinet level office towards becoming an independent agency. As a leading expert argued,

> Social Security has become so big, so complex, and so important in the economy that a Cabinet Secretary does not have adequate time to devote to the many financial, actuarial, statistical and policy issues which arise from the size and nature of the program, and at the same time devote attention to the innumerable controversial other health and welfare problems which are also within the province of Health and Human Services… It is essential for Congress to make changes in the organizational structure of the program. (Cohen, 1984)

Social Security came full circle when it once again became an independent agency in 1995. The debates on whether it should be returned to independent status began in 1981, when the National Commission on Social Security raised the issue, outlining several options for making Social Security into an independent agency. This led to several legislative proposals, and the Social Security Independence and Program Improvement Act of 1994 (P.L. 103-296) was passed by Congress and signed into law on August 14, 1994 by President Clinton (Schieber and Shoven, 1999). On March 31, 1995, the SSA became independent of the Department of Health and Human Service.

Throughout the SSA there exists a process for identifying and implementing key agency initiatives, and these are compiled into one document, the business plan. With the introduction of the yearly accountability report, the agency can track the agency objectives on an annual basis. These reports also enable the agency to comply with the GPRA. For the first time, there was an agency-wide strategic plan in place.

The core processes of the agency are enumeration, earnings, claims, postentitlement, informing the public, and the service delivery interface. The agency's strategic plan long-term goals are:

1. Responsive programs: to promote valued, strong, and responsive Social Security programs and conduct effective policy development, research, and program evaluation;

2.   World-class service: to deliver customer responsive, world class service;

3.   Program management: to make SSA program management the best in the business, with zero

         tolerance for fraud and abuse;

4.   Valued employees: to be an employer that values and invests in each employee; and

5.   To strengthen public understanding of the Social Security program.

         As part of the process of achieving these long-term goals, the agency formulated three short-term

         goals:

1.   To rebuild confidence in Social Security;

2.   To provide world-class service; and

3.   To create a supportive environment for employees. (SSA, 1995c)

The agency has learned the importance of commitment from its leadership and the need to

communicate the plan to all parts of the organization. With the strategic plan, the business plan, and their

association to the budget, the agency is making a statement about where and what is intended to be

accomplished with the public's money. As an internal guidance document, these plans enable decision

makers to steer a consistent course and clarify the SSA's focus and operational vision for the future.

The SSA has a long tradition of measuring the work it does. Over the years, measurements were

created to focus on workloads and performance, primarily concerned with inputs and outputs of the process

but also related to process and program outcomes. For example, along with measuring the numbers of cases

processed and the size of pending workloads, Social Security also measures the number of people whose

incomes Social Security benefits raise above the poverty level and the proportion of administrative

expenditures to program expenditures. Social Security participated in a pilot program to test a new

reporting format that would permit agencies to combine a number of reporting requirements into a single

document. The first such accountability report was published in December 1995 (SSA, 1995c).

In 1996, the Contract with America Advancement Act (P.L. 104-121) made a fundamental change in

the basic philosophy of the disability program. New applicants for Social Security or Supplemental Security

Income disability benefits were no longer eligible for benefits if drug addiction or alcoholism was a material

factor leading to their disability. Previous policy had been that if a person had a medical condition that prevented them from working, they qualified as disabled regardless of the cause of the disability (Schieber and Shoven, 1999).

The Act also eliminated the "comparable severity standard" and reference to "maladapative behavior" in the determination of disability for children's eligibility to receive Supplemental Security Income, and children currently receiving benefits under the old standards were to be revisited and removed from the rolls if they could not qualify under the new standards. SSI eligibility for most non-citizens also was terminated.

Other changes made during the 1996-1997 session required that all federal payments be made electronically effective January 1, 1999, unless a waiver is granted by the Secretary of the Treasury. Supplemental Security Income sponsorship agreements were made legally enforceable for the first time. In the summer of 1997, Congress restored Supplemental Security Income eligibility to certain cohorts of non-citizens, and extended for up to one year the period for redetermining the eligibility of certain aliens who may ultimately not be eligible for continued benefits (Schieber and Shoven, 1999).

From the very beginning, the Social Security program has had the services of periodic advisory councils composed primarily of non-government members whose functions are to represent the public-at-large in advising government officials on Social Security policy. The first such advisory council was convened in 1934 in support of the work of the Committee on Economic Security. Over the years, the advisory councils have been very influential in shaping Social Security. The councils were especially influential in shaping the pivotal 1939 and 1950 amendments. Eventually, the tradition of periodic Social Security advisory councils was made a provision of the law, with a requirement that such a council be appointed every four years. This law stayed in effect until 1994, when it was repealed as part of the legislation that made SSA an independent agency. The 1994 law abolished the councils and substituted a permanent seven-member advisory board to serve many of the same functions. The 1994-1996 advisory council was thus the final council, signaling the end of a long tradition in Social Security and the beginning of the debate on Social Security's future (Ball, 1998). The final advisory council addressed this problem and put forward three competing scenarios for the future:

1.   *Maintain Benefits Plan*, which would keep Social Security essentially as it is, with minor tax increases and benefits reductions along with the possibility of investing some Social Security Trust Fund assets in the private equity market;

2.   *Individual Accounts Plan*, which would add a new mandatory, 1.6% payroll tax to Social Security that would be used to fund an individual investment account managed by the government; and

3.   *Personal Saving Account Plan*, which would partially privatize Social Security by diverting a portion of the payroll tax into individually-managed equity accounts. (Advisory Council on Social Security, 1997)

The Social Security Debate: 1998-2000

These different proposals led to the beginning of a vigorous public debate on the future of the Social Security program. Social Security has always been the focus of intense public interest, and the history of the Social Security program is full of both successes and controversies. Once again political conflict has arisen from the expected changes, as demographic shifts, medical advances, technological advances and budget limitations once again have led to concerns about the future solvency of the Social Security program. Indeed, some of the program's successes have led to some of the biggest challenges. The political debate now turns toward finding the consensus and political will to reform SSA in order to meet the challenges of the new millennium.

The country has grown in population tremendously since the inception of the Social Security program. Medical advances and increases in the standard of living have increased life expectancy as well as the quality of life. However, this has produced an increasing burden for Social Security as more individuals receive benefits for a longer period, creating an impossible strain on the program. The aging of Americans, the so-called "graying of America," means more resources must go toward public and private pensions, medical care, and other social services. How can America prepare and pay for the growing dependency of our rapidly aging population? Under our current Social Security system, our nation cannot meet these obligations (Peterson, 1996). Figures 3.5 Security system, our nation cannot meet these obligations (Peterson, 1996). Figures 3.5 and 3.6 show the number of work to beneficiaries is falling and the aging of the baby boomers.

Figure 3.5 The Number of Workers Per Beneficiary Is Falling

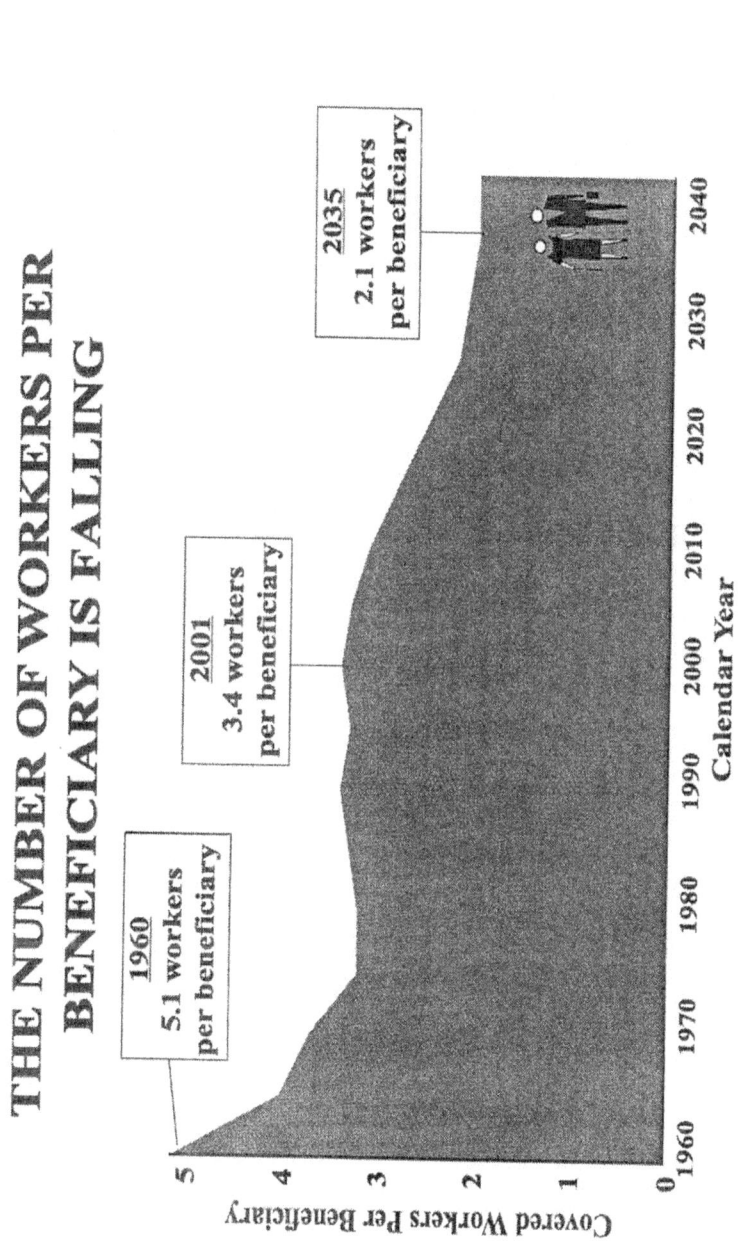

THE NUMBER OF WORKERS PER BENEFICIARY IS FALLING

1960
5.1 workers
per beneficiary

2001
3.4 workers
per beneficiary

2035
2.1 workers
per beneficiary

Covered Workers Per Beneficiary

Calendar Year

THE CONCORD COALITION

Source: Social Security Trustees' Report, March 2001—Intermediate Projections.

Figure 3.6 The Baby Boomers And The U.S. Population in 1960, 1990, 2030

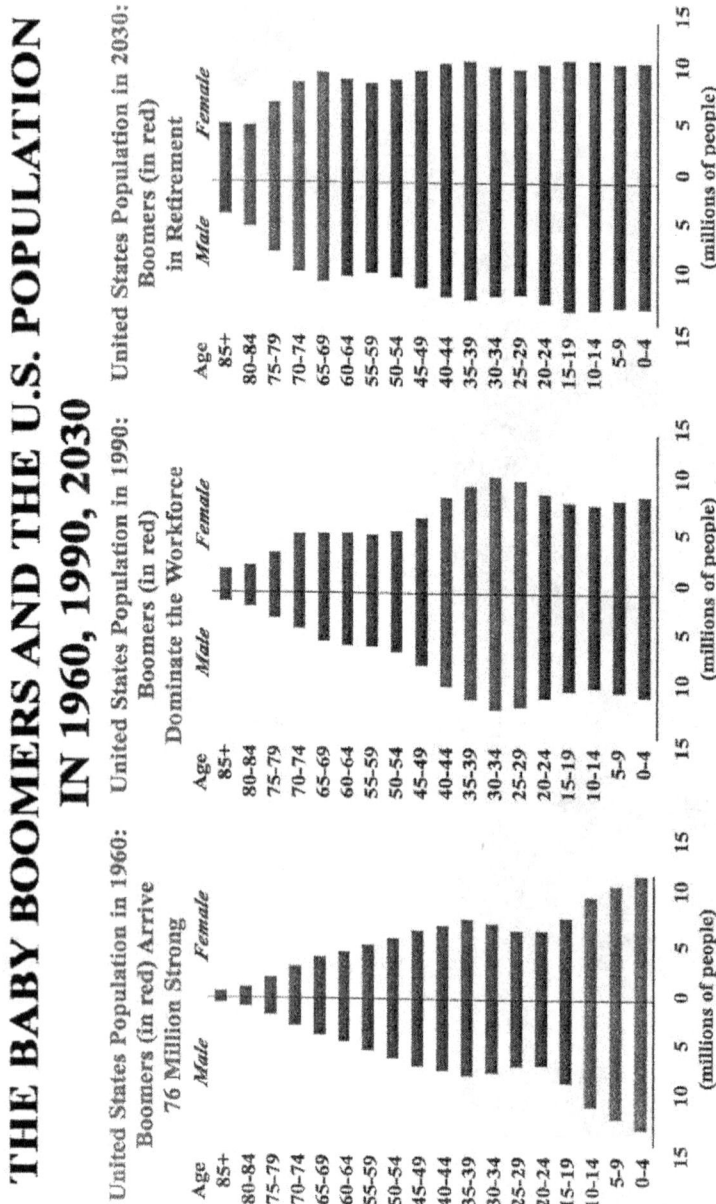

THE BABY BOOMERS AND THE U.S. POPULATION IN 1960, 1990, 2030

Source: U.S. Census Bureau

With the huge increases in budget deficits of the 1980s, the 1990s served as a more conservative time for funding government programs. There were cuts in all areas, which limited increases in the Social Security budget for both administration and programs. The agency suffered from a combination of an incremental increase of responsibilities and a decreased amount of resources with which to fulfill them. This budgetary shift placed an enormous amount of pressure on the agency to improve its performance.

The GPRA and the NPR were two ways in which the legislative and executive branches attempted to guide the ailing bureaucracy.

The advent of the information age has enabled the agency to be innovative in using technology for administering the program. However, it has also increased the expectations of the American public. Social Security has taken the lead in establishing a strong presence on the World Wide Web as another way for the public to seek assistance. Social Security was one of the first federal agencies to focus on possible problems from the Y2K change. Many older Americans have taken advantage of the economic opportunities created by technological advances to extend their work life beyond the traditional retirement age, which has had an impact on the Social Security retirement program. The Social Security number also has become an integral part of keeping records, and is used by the IRS, local governments, credit card companies, and educational institutions. Since the introduction of Social Security, $5.5 trillion has been received and over $4.9 trillion has been paid out. The program has never contributed to the budget deficit, and in fact has enabled the government to fund other projects. Without Social Security, the government would have to find these revenues from other sources (Ball, 1998, p. 4).

For an understanding of the Social Security Trust fund, a review of the evolution of the funding of Social Security must be explored. Under the original Social Security Act of 1935, the funding of social security came from payroll taxes, with the taxing provisions given in Title VIII. As part of the changes in 1939, the taxing provisions were taken from the Social Security Act and inserted in the Internal Revenue Code as the Federal Insurance Contributions Act (FICA). This money collected goes toward administrative costs and paying benefits, with the surpluses to be placed in an "Old Age Reserve Account" and invested in government securities or in securities guaranteed by the government. In the 1939 reforms, a formal Trust Fund was established for the Social Security surpluses. In 1956 the Disability Trust Fund was added to Social Security, and in 1965 a Trust Fund was established for the new Medicare program (SSA, 1998a).

In all but eleven years since 1937, the revenue from FICA taxes has exceeded the benefits paid out, and for those years in which there was a shortfall the reserves were used to pay the difference. Since the surplus is invested in government securities, the money is effectively used to fund other government operations (SSA, 1998a). From 1937 until 1969, the government accounted for the Social Security Trust

Fund separately from the general tax revenue. Beginning in 1969, the Johnson administration used a unified budget, showing all government transactions in one combined budget thus minimizing the budget deficit. This accounting procedure was used until 1986, when the trust funds were once again separated from the general budget. Presently two different budgets are reported, one a unified budget and one which does not include the trust funds. However, this is only an accounting device and has no effect on the actual Social Security budget (Graetz and Mashaw, 1999).

From its inception, Social Security was expected to keep up with the ever-changing needs of society, while at the same time coping with unexpected demographic trends such as the impending retirement of the baby boomers. Social Security makes long range assumptions. The system is projected to have long-range funding problems, and public skepticism about its future persists. Although currently the system's income exceeds its outlays, its board of trustees projected that, on average, over the next 75 years its expenditures will exceed its income by 16% and by 2032 its trust funds will be depleted. The adverse outlook is mirrored by public opinion polls, in which fewer than 50% of the respondents express confidence that the system will be able to meet its long-range commitments. There is also a growing awareness that Social Security will not be as good a value in the future as it is for today's retirees. Until recent years, a typical retiree could expect to receive far more in benefits than he or she paid in Social Security taxes. However, because Social Security tax rates have increased and the age for receipt of full benefits is scheduled to rise from 65 to 67, it has been increasingly apparent that the system will be less favorable for future recipients (Congressional Research Service, 1998).

After the creation of the SSA, the program scrambled to stay afloat and develop into the program we know today. The evolution of this bureaucracy serves as a reflection of how this program was transformed from a vague concept into an important entitlement as changes were enacted by Congress, extending the program's responsibilities. This more comprehensive program required more personnel and bureaucratic infrastructure to reach every American worker. Thomas P. (Tip) O'Neil (D-MA), former Speaker of the House, called Social Security the "third rail of American Politics" (O'Neil, 1987). This elevated Social Security programs to the status of "sacred cows" that were not to be tampered with, regardless of the consequences. Because the elderly are better organized and turn out to vote in large numbers, they speak with a strong voice that is heard by the elected officials who deal with public programs.

In the 1990's, a looming crisis arose which pitted the baby boomers against the Generation Xers (Coupland, 1991). Political leaders were debating the need to reform the program to keep it solvent for the next generation of beneficiaries, as there are not enough current and future workers to sustain the promised level of benefits for current and future social security recipients. A much-cited poll showed that a majority of individuals under 25 had a stronger belief in the existence of UFOs than in the future solvency of Social Security (Luntz Research Company, 1994). Two fiscal realities, and the demographic trend underlying them, are the primary causes of this seismic shift. When the Roosevelt Administration created Social Security, the life expectancy was lower than the retirement age it established. Now 31.2 million Americans, or 12.6 % of the population, are over 65. In 1945, 45 workers were paying into the system for every retiree drawing benefits. Now that ratio is 3:1. By 2030 it is projected to be close to 2:1. If current benefits and taxes are maintained, the program will go broke. (Ponnuru, 1997). The solution to this dilemma is simple: either taxes must be increased or benefits cut. Either way, it presents tough political choices.

In President Clinton's 1998 State of the Union Address, he vowed to "save Social Security first." The prospect of projected increasing budget surpluses, coupled with a state of peace and economic prosperity, led attempts to focus the national dialogue on finding a new solution for the looming social security crisis (Broder, 1998). Clinton proposed a series of regional meetings sponsored by various groups and the Congress that would serve as a means to educate the public and find alternative solutions to the problem which would be acceptable to the American people. These meetings would conclude with a National Conference on Social Security to be held at the White House in December 1998.

Unfortunately, shifts in the political landscape, such as the President's impeachment, congressional leadership change, and the 2000 Presidential election cycle resulted in a missed opportunity for solving the complex issues facing Social Security. The decisions needed inevitably impacted an important interest group or constituency in a negative way.

The number of interest groups attempting to maintain the status quo are numerous, and include the National Committee to Preserve Social Security and the American Association of Retired People. There is an equally wide range of organizations calling for major reform. Of particular importance is the Concord Coalition, a nonpartisan group pushing for radical reform which was founded by former Senators Rudman, Tsongas, and Nunn. The Concord Coalition is largely concerned with budgetary issues and the importance of educating the public. Other organizations, such as the Cato Institute, advocate the total elimination of the federal program and its replacement by private sector organizations.

Any reform of the system needs to take into account the impact it would have on the initial intent of the program (to provide financial protection for the elderly), the economic and federal budget, and the administrative costs of implementation. The agreement for current and near-future retirees must be preserved, but for future beneficiaries, the level of benefits which will be available is more uncertain. The SSA is standing at the crossroads of its most crucial decision since its inception in 1935.

Conclusion

This chapter addresses the catalyst that enabled the creation of SSA and the changes within its legislative evolution. What makes SSA a unique government organization is that programs were added throughout its organizational existence that created eras of both expansion and stagnation. The organizational structure has had to shift and change to meet the expanding demands from its competing constituencies. In SSA's life history, it currently has reached a stable level of maturity and is at a crossroads. The tough challenges facing SSA are how to continue to provide the coverage promised to several generations of beneficiary without bankrupting the program. The next chapter addresses the enactment and evolution of the National Partnership for Reinvention (NPR) and its attempt to make government "work better and cost less" by "reinventing it."

Chapter 4 National Partnership for Reinvention (NPR)

"Our goal is to make the entire federal government both less expensive and more efficient, and to change the culture of our national bureaucracy away from complacency and entitlement toward initiative and empowerment. We intend to redesign, to reinvent, and to reinvigorate the entire national government."

President Bill Clinton, announcing NPR, March 3, 1993.

The Social Security Administration (SSA) is a complex federal bureaucracy that provides a basic level of social insurance for most working Americans. The Social Security program has evolved significantly since its inception in 1935 in response to the constant challenges it has experienced due to the shifting demands and needs of both the public and elected officials. The National Partnership for Reinvention (NPR) was designed to make government "work better and cost less" based on criticism arising from the public's generally low opinion of the federal government (*Washington Post*, 1993 Gore, 1993, p. 1). This policy was an attempt to facilitate change within the federal government. The perception is that the federal government is a highly bureaucratic system whereas the private sector operates in the global technological information age. A drastic transformation is needed and NPR is the vehicle of change. This policy can be categorized as part of a much larger continual focus on federal government reforms, of which there have been at least eleven in the last 100 years. NPR had its origins in the 1992 presidential campaign and was an attempt to "reinvent government," especially within SSA. This chapter focuses primarily on the phases of evolution of the NPR Policy and how it relates to SSA.

History of Governmental Reforms

Reorganizing, restructuring, and overall reform is not a new process for the federal government. In the late 1800s, the discipline of public administration evolved on the premise of bringing professionalism to the federal government (Wilson, 1887). To function well, a government requires constant evaluation and review in order to prevent the stagnation inherent in bureaucracies. Consequently, over the last one hundred years there has been a long history of attempts to deal with growth and changes in the federal structure.

Preoccupation with executive reorganization has been a major focus of 11 of the last 17 presidents to take office. Most government reform efforts were based on three major ideas: (a) a doctrine of democratic accountability, (b) improved business efficiency, and/or (c) the expansion of presidential policy leadership (Wilson, 1994). What these three goals had in common was a focus on the institutional and political interests of the incumbent president.

The attempts to reform government span the major efforts of the 1937 Brownlow Commission and the two Hoover Commissions (1947-49 and 1953-55), which were the most wide-reaching, being devoted to an overall review of the organization and function of the executive branch. In 1972, after a thorough review, the Nixon administration proposed to consolidate seven departments into four. Most recently, in the Reagan administration, the Grace Commission, 1982-84, focused entirely on shrinking the size of government and improving efficiency (Kettl and DiIulio, 1995).

NPR has been credited for having the most aggressive management reform program in history (Kettl, 1994). What has made NPR different from other efforts is that it is comprised of federal employees who work within the systems they are attempting to reform. Non-governmental experts from outside the culture and organizational structure of the federal government headed previous government reform programs. With the benefit of their inside knowledge, the civil servants hoped to accomplish much more than previous commissions because they were not only recommending changes but had a real sense of what was possible and were able to return to their agencies and put many of the recommendations into practice. This use of federal employees was also very helpful in convincing government agencies to accept the proposals rather than simply dismissing them as another passing fad by the political leadership. Government reform initiatives are known for being short lived, owing partly to the short attention spans of politicians (March and Olsen, 1989). The unique perspective of NPR meant that they had the political and administrative support in place to facilitate the implementation of the proposed recommendations. This advantage opened a window of opportunity within the federal bureaucracy in which it was receptive to change.

This most recent attention to reinvention has been longer lived than many of its predecessors, for a variety of reasons. First, the two terms of the Clinton administration have allowed the program time to mature and for the reforms to have some effect. Another is the Vice President's commitment to and identification with the policy of reinvention.

The 1992 Presidential Campaign

During the 1992 presidential campaign, Bill Clinton and Al Gore traveled extensively, addressing town meetings across America. The feedback they received from voters regarding their dissatisfaction with the federal government served as a catalyst for the creation of NPR. At the same time, Osborne and Gabler wrote about the overwhelming need to change and create a more entrepreneurial style of government. The authors support public administration on all levels, professing a belief that a civilized society cannot function without effective government. Osborne and Gabler point out that the people who work in government are not necessarily the problem; it is the system within which they must operate that is flawed. The challenges faced by the federal and state governments are not necessarily related to traditional conservatism or liberalism; the major concern is and should be equity and the provision of equal opportunity for all Americans (Osborne and Gabler, 1993, p. xix). This book cites examples of entrepreneurial government at the state and locals levels that show how government officials can be creative and innovative in providing services for the public. The combination of the victory of the Clinton/Gore campaign and the push for governmental reform set the scene for the creation of the NPR.

The National Performance Review (NPR)

In *Putting People First* (1992), President Clinton and Vice President Gore wrote about how focusing on reforming government would change the public's perception toward government and make government more customer driven. On March 3, 1993, President Clinton created the NPR and appointed the Vice-President as leader of the task force. David Osborne, author of *Reinventing Government* (1993), was a key advisor to the task force, which included over 250 career civil servants. The group was divided into two teams, one that focused on individual agencies and the other on government-wide systems. In addition to these external objectives, the President directed agencies to create internal reinvention teams and establish areas of innovation that could be granted waivers from internal agency rules (Gore, 1993).

What set NPR apart from earlier government reform efforts was that this group was largely composed of federal civil servants, rather than individuals from outside the government. These individuals had worked inside the federal bureaucracy and understood the conflicts and tensions found in government. They benefited from their personal experience working within the confines of the federal government and were able to propose changes that both were necessary and attainable.

The Vice President took part in an extensive series of "town hall" meetings in several agencies, opening a dialogue about the problems facing each agency. In June 1993, a "Reinvention Summit" was held in which government leaders, consultants, and business leaders met to talk about dealing with changes and innovation. The Vice President met with each agency head to garner support for the NPR. He also directed the NPR staff to target the overhead cost rather than the organizational structure of agencies; the recommendations should deal with administrative changes, not statutory changes.

The final report, *Creating a Government that Works Better and Cost Less,* was presented to President Clinton by Vice President Gore on September 7, 1993 and made 384 Recommendations. The recommendations were based on 38 additional reports detailing 1,250 specific action items and intended to save over $108 billion over five years. It also focused on reducing the number of management positions and improving government operations (Gore, 1993). With the completion of this report, there were now specific examples of what reforms were needed in order to meet the objectives set by NPR.

The President and Vice President traveled the country to promote the report. President Clinton issued directives to implement a number of recommendations, which included cutting the work force by 252,000 positions and creating a 15 to 1 ratio of employees to management. Other areas focused on cutting regulations in half and requiring agencies to set customer service standards (Gore, 1993). The approach used to present the findings was similar to a town hall meeting. They were held across the country in every imaginable location. There was a cross section of federal employees and they were allowed to add suggestions to the proposed ones. This was very effective in spreading the message that NPR was going to empower all federal employees.

Simultaneously, Congress, working on similar government reforms, adopted the Government Performance Results Act (GPRA) of 1993 which mandated that agencies develop strategic and performance plans and publish performance measures annually. Government agencies now were accountable for their annual appropriations based on performance measurements (Gore, 1993). What was unique in the application of the NPR proposals was that the Republican congressional members could agree on the proposals. They resonated on the side of the Republican's theme of what was wrong in government.

NPR was not without its critics; the Republicans were skeptical of this reform movement (Grassley, 1993), as was the academic community (Hart, 1997). The near absence of any reference to democratic accountability is perhaps the most striking feature of the Gore report (Wilson, 1994). Some critics dismissed this program as another hollow proposal full of political rhetoric and so-called "reforms" that endangered the public trust (Kettl, 1994), while others thought the focus of "reinvention" should have been on the purpose and relationship of government with all levels of government and non-government sector organizations (Drucker, 1995b). The NPR also was criticized for its tendency to focus on savings rather than improvements in performance and because many of the successes cited are programs that the agencies already had in place. Lastly, this effort was criticized due to its origins within the executive branch and its lack of a cohesive plan to involve Congress in the process of reinvention (Kettl, 1994).

Phase I: Implementing the Reinvention of Government

NPR changed its focus from looking for ways to reform the federal bureaucracy towards actually turning the recommendations into action items. Once the report was presented, most of the staff returned to their home federal agencies, leaving 50 staff members to start implementing and following the initiatives set forth (Kamensky, 1999). A campaign to communicate the message of reinvention was taken to the federal work force, particularly its focus on cutting red tape, putting customers first, empowering employees to get results, and getting back to basics (Gore, 1993). The most critical challenge was to communicate the ideas represented by NPR to the entire federal government community.

The tool used to recognize the agencies that were leading the way in setting a new standard of achievement was the "Hammer Award," which was designed to represent how government was moving closer to its ideal of working better and costing less. The Hammer symbolized yesterday's government and the much cited $400 cost when the government bought hammers, and consisted of a $6.00 hammer, a ribbon, and a note from the Vice President, all in an aluminum frame. At the presentation ceremonies, lapel "hammers" were also awarded to recognize the contributions of outstanding individuals (Walker, 1997). The criteria of the award is competitive and allows any federal agency to apply for and receive recognition for real innovation.

Phase II: Redefining Reinvention

With a Republican majority in the Congress in the winter of 1995, President Clinton directed the Vice President to launch the second phase of reinvention. The emphasis of this reform was primarily on what government should be doing, but it was also intended to include an assessment of how well it was working. In September 1995, over 200 more recommendations were proposed which would save an extra $70 billion dollars over five years. NPR touted a savings of over $58 billion from the $108 billion in savings that were originally projected (Kamensky, 1999). The objectives during this time period were to deal with reforms in the regulatory system, and to review programs in agencies that could be eliminated entirely. Benchmark studies were conducted that focused on specific issues. In a separate analysis, a Customer

Service Standards report showed that over 3,000 standards of service to the public were found in 214 agencies.

One example of a successful innovation was the use of tele-service within SSA (NPR, 1995). An independent study by the Dalbar, Inc. group rated the Social Security 800 number as a leader in providing customer service, ranking them higher than Norstrom, L.L. Bean and many other top companies (Harvey and DiCesare, 1995). The NPR also used performance agreements in place of restrictive grant programs for its work with state and local governments to facilitate dealing with the red tape and improve services.

Agency performance was not the only area that NPR focused its attention. As part of Congress's move towards achieving a balanced budget, Vice President Gore outlined new initiatives designed to deal with the limitations that would result. These were wide ranging, and mainly were concerned with how more decisions were going to be moved to the front line. The government should focus on the ends rather than the means and make agencies more performance based, with improved use of customer services and the increased use of regulatory partnerships (Gore, 1996). Once these initiatives had been defined, teams were put in place that were able to focus on their implementation.

Reinvention in the Second Clinton Administration

To disseminate more widely the successes of individual departments produced by the NPR initiative, the administration wanted to share the insights found by the individual agencies. Cabinet secretaries and heads of other government agencies, met at Blair House to discuss which parts of the program had worked best for their particular organizations. This sharing of ideas resulted in the *Blair House Papers* (Human Development Council, 1997), which were produced as a means of publicizing the tools of reinvention. Another step taken to ensure that these ideas became more widely known was the development of a booklet by the Human Resource Development Council that enabled the ideas found in the *Blair House Papers* to be more easily implemented within agencies. Every agency was to teach their administrative heads using the principles found in the booklet, *Getting Results Through Learning*. Thus, the ideas were spread government-wide and provided a basis for the creation of some standards by which to

measure the successes found in implementing NPR (Gore, 1997).

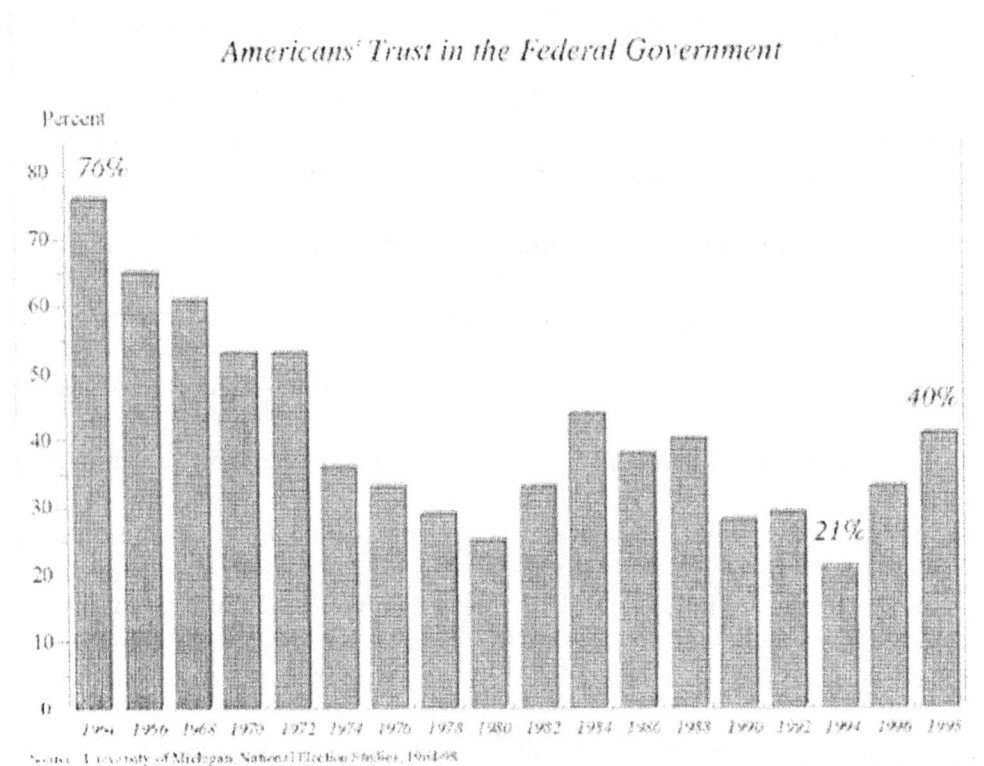

Americans' Trust in the Federal Government

Percent

80 | 76%

70

60

50

40   40%

30

20   21%

10

0

1964 1966 1968 1970 1972 1974 1976 1978 1980 1982 1984 1986 1988 1990 1992 1994 1996 1998

Source: University of Michigan, National Election Studies, 1964-98

Figure 4.1

The successes of NPR were significant. According to public opinion polls, public trust was up from a 30

year low as can be seen in the chart. The University of Michigan, which has conducted surveys biannually

for the past 40 years asked, "Do you trust the Federal Government to do the right things most of the time?"

76 percent of Americans expressed confidence in the Federal Government in 1964. By 1994, that number

had declined to only 21 percent. By late 1998, it had risen to 40 percent. There was no direct link between

the NPR and the poll, but the Clinton administration took credit for some of that shift. The most dramatic

change was that the federal civilian workforce was the smallest since 1931 as a percentage of the national

workforce. Between 1993 and 1995 over 1,500 actions were recommended, with the agencies completing

about 58 percent. Of the original set of recommendations, 66 percent had been completed. President

Clinton had signed 46 directives, which Congress passed, and over 85 new laws. The Hammer Award was

given to over 1,200 federal teams, and over 350 "reinvention labs" had created pilot innovations. Hammer

Award winners were credited with savings of over $31 billion. Overall, the original projected savings from the two rounds was $177 billion over 5 years, and agencies had locked in about $137 billion of these savings. Agencies also eliminated over 640,000 pages of internal rules and 16,000 pages of Federal Regulations, and had rewritten 31,000 additional pages into "plain language" (Kamensky, 1999).

Phase III: National Partnership for Reinvention (NPR)

In March 1998, a celebration was held to mark the fifth anniversary of the creation of NPR. With the success of the initial phase of the NPR movement, a decision was made to expand the effort and reinvent the National Performance Review itself. The name was changed to the National Partnership for Reinvention and it was reorganized. In essence, the initiative did to itself what it advocated government-wide.

With these changes, the biggest challenge facing the program remained the conversion of traditional, hierarchical industrial age bureaucracies to high performance, information age organizations. The next step was to take the existing successes and extend them across the entire federal structure. Another unfinished challenge was to change the basic "rules of the game" in the government bureaucracy and tackle its budgetary, personnel, and management systems (Kamensky, 1999).

One of the most significant successes of the NPR is the reduction in size of the federal government, which shrank by 351,000 employees between January 1993 and January 1998. The United States government now has its smallest civilian workforce since President John F. Kennedy held office, and the smallest percentage of the national workforce since 1961. When compared with the completion rates of previous reform efforts, such as the Hoover and Grace Commissions, the NPR made outstanding progress in terms of the traditional measures of reform and the number of recommendations enacted. However, even with the countless positive affirmations, critics have argued that the reforms have not been real and significant changes but minor cosmetic ones.

As discussed, NPR has been promoted as an example of how the Clinton Administration has been effective in implementing organizational change within the federal government. In its short-lived history,

NPR has been a part of a public relations campaign promoting how government "works better and cost less" under the Clinton administration. However, criticisms have arisen from the NPR policy and they do merit a brief discussion and evaluation in this section.

The most often cited criticism of NPR is that the "reinventing government" movement is not a new government reform but a continuation of every new administration's attempt to fix all the wrongs of government (Norris, 2000). These previous reforms have been thinly veiled with political ideology while masquerading under different management reform models. Some even have stated that attempts to reforming the public sector are almost as old as the nation itself. One can even argue that the very creation of the country is built on a tradition of change or reinvention beginning with the revolution of 1776 (Lutrin and Shani, 1998). In the last 100 years, every new presidential administration has focused on reorganizing the federal bureaucracy. NPR is a potpourri of attempts of previous government reform movements and is excessively optimistic about the prospects for changing the way that government does business (Norris, 2000). This political naiveté adds to the cynicism found toward the business of government (Gazell, 1997).

This criticism is easy to assert but society is continually changing and evolving, government needs to be able to adapt to the shifting needs of the public. Thus, these government reform movements enable incremental changes to the system. Most reform movements have been able to identify areas of reform and attempt to handle the bureaucracy.

Another criticism is that the NPR has overstated the problems of performance of the federal government and their objectives have been too simplistic (Gazell, 1997). By doing so, targets can meet the low expectations and allow the bureaucrats to repackage and present initiatives as "reinvention" success when in reality they were simply more of the same. This criticism feeds off the cynicism of the Washington culture of playing the political game of moving shells around. NPR may be simplistic, but it is what has made the policy so effective. This policy was also a beginning to a much larger attempt to reform government.

Critics also cite that the proposals established by NPR fail to recommend how to reduce government in an effective means. Furthermore, it also fails to examine what structure is needed for the proposals to succeed and the organizational shortcomings of existing ones (Golembiewski, 1997). Many of the changes cited by NPR movement could not be accomplished solely by the executive branch and require legislative intervention. NPR should have addressed a much broader area such as how the public sector redefines the relationship between the federal, state, and local government with non-government sectors (Drucker, 1995b). This is a much larger issue and one policy leaders have failed to address. The problems dealing with the federal government did not develop over night and the solutions certainly will take an equal amount of time.

Critics also point out that the values of government cannot be compared to the values of the private sector. The paradigm of the public sector uses a different model than what is found within the private sector (Hart, 1997). The democratic process is slow and government is geared toward accountability not empowerment. The shifting of government officials from implementation of laws enacted by representatives of citizens toward one of the satisfaction of customers preferences which are frequently volatile (Gazell, 1997) is not an example of good government. They lack a long-term focus and do hinder the responsibilities of government. This argument does merit some consideration but lessons found with organizations, either public or private can be applied accordingly. NPR is the beginning of a continual evaluation of the administration of government.

Another obstacle to NPR is that the federal government structure is too complex to change significantly in one president's tenure in office. The frailties of government pointed out by NPR are presented in a much simpler way than they actually are. Guy (1997) has pointed to seven variables whose presence in federal agencies work against the likelihood in creating change: culture, trust, structure, organizational behavior, work force composition, partisan politics, and routine. By over promising with results or huge fiscal savings, NPR has misrepresented its assertions. Some of the reforms of financial savings base these findings on accounting tricks and do not measure up. A recent 1999 General Accounting report harshly criticized NPR as being merely much ado about nothing, whose savings were not as significant as claimed (GAO, 1999). This also can be countered by realizing that NPR is a part of a continual effort to reform government.

Finally, another criticism is that NPR is really a thinly veiled attempt to raise Vice President Gore's stature within the administration. The role of a Vice President is very limited and can be a bad position for someone with presidential aspirations. By heading NPR, Gore was able to showcase the policy and bring recognition to his abilities of leadership and political savvy within the federal government. NPR was also a hodgepodge of recommendations and superficial manipulation of reform for political advantage (Moe, 1994; Arnold, 1995).

In addition, all NPR task forces carry significant political clout. The physical location of the NPR offices is across the street from the White House. This close relationship with the administration brings clout and facilitates encouraging bureaucrats to meet the expectations established by NPR. Federal managers have been, at best, mixed and most are very cynical of these reforms movements (Sweeny and Hyde, 1995). Even with this appearance of posturing by the Vice President, it did raise the stature of the efforts on reforming government to be taken seriously.

Implementing NPR Within the Social Security Administration (SSA)

The NPR initiative and the Social Security Administration (SSA) have enjoyed a close working relationship. In promoting reinvention, the NPR creates public systems that act very differently from the bureaucracies the American people have come to know. It creates organizations that can compete with the best commercial customer service departments in the business, as the SSA did in 1995 with its telephone service, providing services in a form which their customers can most easily use (Osborne and Plastrick, 1997).

The SSA relationship with the NPR was a perfect match for several reasons. The SSA's responsibilities are primarily to their customers, dealing directly with individuals as they move toward meeting the agency's objectives. Another important factor was the decision by then Commissioner Shirley

Chater to use these initiatives as a method to gain favor and insight into the administration (Chater, 1997). She reasoned that cabinet and independent agencies compete among themselves to get the attention of the executive branch, particularly the President, in order to improve their standing in the national political agenda and benefit from the President's persuasive powers (Neustadt, 1965; Reich, 1997). This emphasis by the President would assist the Social Security Administration in a host of arenas, such as securing additional appropriations from the Congress, expanding administrative authority, or simply enhancing the stature of the political appointees, enabling them to deal with the bureaucracy more effectively (Heclo, 1977).

As a result of this thinking, the SSA embraced the policy initiatives set forth by the NPR, seeking to implement and take a lead in making this program work within the agency. Internally, SSA created a new position in the commissioner's office to be the person specifically responsible for the NPR initiatives (Chater, 1997). This individual would report directly to the Commissioner of Social Security and be part of the executive staff. The agency also loaned out several government executives, known as detailees, to be the first task group to work on the first wave of government-wide recommendations.

To implement the NPR, recommendations required changes to be made to the organizational architecture of federal agencies, which presented a major challenge to the highly bureaucratic SSA. The changes were intended to flatten hierarchies and delete mid-management positions, changing the way decisions are made and who makes them, the form of communication, and accountability standards. These changes have implications that are far more wide-reaching than mere enhancement of productivity. In the case of SSA, it focused on what Gore said was the "root problem" of contemporary government, namely its reliance on "large, top-down, centralized bureaucracies." The solution was to create "entreprenuerial organizations," by which is meant organizations that "constantly learned, innovated, and improved" (Wilson, 1994).

The transition to independent agency status was also cited as a Reinvention initiative. SSA had been a part of the Department of Health and Human Services, which represented the agency at the cabinet level. This move to independence had been advocated for many years, but had been blocked by serious political obstacles. The move to independent agency status came as part of President Clinton's effort to gain

support for his health care program. In order to get the support of Senator Daniel P. Moynihan (D-NY),

the President pledged to support legislation allowing Social Security to become an independent agency

(Chater, 1997). Once it had been signed into law, President Clinton announced:

> With an independent SSA, we are reinventing our Government to streamline our operations
>
> so that we can serve the American people better. We are strengthening those things which
>
> Social Security ought to do and taking precautions to make sure it does not do things which
>
> it ought not to do. It is proving that Government can still work to improve people's lives.
>
> And now Social Security, we know, will work better" (Clinton, 1994).

As a result of becoming an independent agency, the Social Security Administration was now able to

deal directly with the President and distance itself from other controversial programs found within the

Department of Health and Human Services.

The need for reform of government must always be kept in mind. Although programs are initially

created to meet a perceived need, the organizations evolve over time and often become more focused on

the people that they employ rather than the people they were created to serve. The federal bureaucracy

serves as a living example of a major problem found in modern day governance: How do you strike a

balance between serving the interests of the public while simultaneously meeting the fiscal responsibilities of

government? The public demands more governmental programs, but hesitates when asked to pay higher

taxes to cover the increased costs of the new services. Effective leaders are able to maximize the resources

allocated for administration of government.

In response to demands for greater accountability, the agency began to redesign its systems to make

them more customer service oriented. Over 40,000 customers were surveyed, and the complaints were

found mostly to concern the long and complex process of applying for disability benefits. The process was

compared to that of a Model T assembly line. Each claim was handled by up to 26 Social Security workers,

requiring over 5 months, before an initial decision was made. If the claim was turned down and the result appealed, as many as 43 workers were involved in processing the claim, taking as much as two and half years. In response, the agency implemented a new system for disability claims, with fewer steps and fewer staff involved, which was created with the customer in mind, and in some cases cut the waiting time down to 20 months.

Other highlights of the customer standards are that when Social Security cards must be issued or replaced, they will be mailed to the recipient within five working days. When appointments are made, customers will be seen within ten minutes of the scheduled time. Customers are told an estimate of the time it will takes to complete a request or expected delays. Decisions are explained in a simple manner, and accompanied by an explanation of the appeals procedure if the customer disagrees with the decision (Gore, 1994a, p. 14).

In 1998, SSA was selected as a high impact agency. The agency made a commitment to achieve a number of significant, concrete, measurable goals. If anyone calls the 800 number, the agency ensures that the call is answered within five minutes at least 95 percent of the time and the public is able to get through to the 800 number at least 90 percent of the time. Each individual working person over 25 is sent an annual statement of their contribution record and an entitlement statement. Employers are able to get overnight electronic verification of the Social Security numbers of each employee, and have the option of transmitting earnings data to the agency electronically. Claims are taken over the phone when applying for retirement or survivor benefits, as long as all the information is available, and notices are sent in response to questions. The bold recommendation to change the payment cycle of Social Security checks was also implemented.

This policy originated at the top levels of the SSA. The real challenge, however, is for the policy objectives to filter down to the ten regional offices and their local district offices intact. This study of the impact of the policy on the Atlanta Regional Office, which oversees ten states and is the largest region within the Social Security Administration, should provide valuable information on whether the NPR created real changes in the organizational effectiveness of the SSA.

The concept of reinvention is based on the principles of flattening the hierarchy, empowering workers to make decisions, using entrepreneurial business methods, and introducing a new agency culture. This change was accomplished by using existing federal workers to be a part of the NPR task force and then returned to their home agencies to spread what they learned. In theory, this would allow "islands" of reinvention to flourish and incrementally change the culture of the agencies. Within SSA, a leadership program was initiated to teach managers how to become leaders and make the agency a "learning organization".

From the beginning, many observers have shared their concerns about how realistic these expectations of achieving substantive reform of the federal government would prove to be. Agency structures only can be altered slowly, and the inevitable inertia tends to dull the edge of real change. For the NPR to be effective federal employees must exercise a degree of freedom far in excess of that generally permitted them by a suspicious populace. Government is not a business, and Americans value the actions of government differently than they value the work of the business sector. The failure to understand this paradox produces simplistic comparisons such as: "If it works in business, it will work in government." This simply is not true. A government that is too responsive fails to provide the checks and balances intended by the framers of our Constitution. Patronage and a return to spoils are currently guarded against by a myriad of rules and procedures. To abandon them certainly will speed up processes, but in the long run the safeguards are likely to be reinstated to satisfy those who do not like government and not want any government worker to have any more discretion than is absolutely essential (Rohr, 1986).

Leadership Styles

On the subject of leadership, Gore acknowledges that power will not decentralize on its own accord: "It must be pushed and pulled out of the hands of the people who have wielded it for so long" (Gore,

1994b, p. *22*). Labor-management partnerships are stressed. He points out that as a result of mistrust, traditional union-employer relations are not well-suited to handling a culture change that asks workers and mangers to think first about the customer and to work hand in hand to improve quality. He considers that government only can be transformed if the adversarial relationship that dominates federal union-management interactions is transformed into a partnership for building a better alliance between employees and managers, thus creating the energy necessary to power change for a long time (Bowsher, 1992).

Other challenges facing government administrators include sunshine laws, sanctions from Congress, and other oversight mechanisms. Political appointees, who are in charge of the agencies, average less than two years in a post, giving their time horizon a short-term focus and imposing a style of management that is risk averse and focused on short term success.

Organizational Culture

Constraints rather than freedoms drive the organizational architecture of the federal government. Constraints are placed on agencies to ensure consistent responses rather than arbitrary decision making. The private sector, unencumbered by having to be accountable to elected officials, has a different architecture. The structures in business organizations are designed to contribute toward the organization's purpose of making a profit. The immediacy of this form of accountability creates the need for maximum flexibility and discretion. Changing accountability requires a culture change that permeates the thinking of employees at all levels as well as the thinking of those who judge government. Unfortunately, the likelihood of this occurring is not great. Organizational culture, like a stretched rubber band, tends to return to its original shape as soon as the tension is released (Kilmann, 1985).

Public Policy Implementation

In the face of cultural resistance, the biggest challenge facing the NPR was implementing the program into all areas of government. Most of the focus of the report was on persuading the leaders at the highest levels of each agency that the White House was serious about achieving real changes in the way the agencies operated and convincing the rank-and-file that the White House "feels their pain." The result so far, in the words of one NPR staffer, are "islands of excellence surrounded by continents of indifference" (Walker, 1997). To make the islands grow and continents shrink, the staff has continuously focused on selling their ideas by example, going from agency to agency with stories of things that have worked in other agencies and promises of protection for those employees who have gone out on a limb to put into effect a procurement reform or a customer-service innovation. Trying to teach by example and anecdote, the staff calls attention to such things as the "Forgiveness coupons" that one federal agency has created to try to assure its employees that taking risks and making mistakes need not destroy a career (Kamensky, 1997).

Short of amending the Constitution or turning back the clock to our pre-pluralist days, there is little that can be done to make customer service the key to public administration. To empower employees, it is necessary first to disempower legislators, judges, and White House staffers, and leave tasks for which customer service is paramount in the private sector. The choice is described best by Wilson: "You can either have big government or you can have government that is easy to deal with and flexible in its management of complexities and problems. But I doubt you can have both." (1994, p. 32).

According to Mazmanian and Sabatier:

[The implementation process] normally runs through a number of stages beginning with passage of the basic statute, followed by the policy outputs (decisions) of the implementing agencies, the compliance of target groups with those decisions, the actual impacts- both intended and unintended – of those outputs, the perceived impacts of agency decisions, and, finally, important revisions in the basic statute. (1983, p. 43)

Pressman and Wildavsky (1973) note that implementation differs from more traditional approaches to public administration because it focuses narrowly on the interaction between setting the goals and the actions taken rather than policy outcomes. Montjoy and O'Toole (1979) offer a similar point of view as they refer to decisions made in carrying out a policy as implementation and the effect on the ultimate target as the impact. Therefore, a central goal of this study is to illustrate the relative strength of administrative capacity and its ability to influence outcomes. To examine the Social Security's administrative capacity in managing the NPR Policy this study's focus will be directed to the following three stages of the implementation process:

Stage 1) Policy outputs of the implementing agencies;

Stage 2) Compliance with policy outputs by target groups; and

Stage 3) Actual impacts of policy outputs.

The central goal of the study is to uncover the various ways in which the policy may have assisted in improving government.

Conclusion

When the Clinton administration was winding down, the final stage focus of NPR was to continue to deliver world class customer service, dramatically increase electronic government, combine outcomes that no one agency can achieve alone and, finally, to imbed reinvention in government's culture.

To make true reinvention work, several architectural elements of government must change substantially. This is why, once the initial fanfare has died down, meaningful change will be difficult to achieve. As Kaufman describes the challenge: "Bureaucracies are stubborn creatures, with personalities and habits of their own. They may jump through a few hoops to please their newest political masters, … reinvention can polish the surface without touching the soul." (1991, p. 156). This is further discussed and analyzed in Chapters Six and Seven.

Chapter 5 Research Methodology

So far, this dissertation has reviewed the literature and provided a brief overview of the Social Security Administration (SSA) and the National Performance Review (NPR) policy initiative. This chapter focuses on the research method utilized in this dissertation, the case study. This approach best meets the objectives of determining if implementation of NPR created organizational change within the Southern Region of the SSA. This study sheds some light on the internal institutional dynamics within the SSA. Specifically, this study seeks to identify the relationships between some of the more important theoretical principles found within the field of public administration. This chapter then discusses the case study methodology, focusing on its strengths and weaknesses. An explanation of how the collection of data was performed, and the selection of the sources and type of information sought is discussed. Finally, the expected findings of the study are summarized.

Theoretical Considerations

This dissertation focuses on one part of the SSA, the Southern Region, and aims to understand the internal dynamics of the organization and how policy is implemented within one region of this huge government bureaucracy. The research specifically addresses core areas within public administration, such as dealing with policy implementation, leadership styles, organizational culture, and organizational change.

These specific areas are important, as they are central to the functions of public administration. By using this analytical framework, scholars are better able to understand the workings of public organizations. Nonetheless, even though this focus can facilitate a general view, it is only a small part of the larger federal bureaucratic structure.

The Case Study Method

This research is a case study involving qualitative techniques using a ground-theory approach. As Yin states, " In general, case studies are the preferred strategy when 'how' or 'why' questions are being posed, when the investigator has little control over events, and when the focus is on a contemporary phenomenon within some real life context." (1989, p. 13).

Qualitative research as a method of data collection and analysis derived from the *Verstehen* tradition. According to the *Verstehen* (German for "empathy") approach, the natural and social sciences are distinct bodies of knowledge because of the divergence in the nature of their subject matter. The process of *Verstehen*, also deemed interpretive understanding, requires one to grasp the categories through which the world is organized (Nachmias and Nachmias, 1992). A researcher who has not been initially socialized into the subject culture must go through a process in order to acquire a sense of the shared meanings within the culture. Scholars in the social sciences must gain an empathetic understanding of societal phenomena, recognizing both the historical dimension of human behavior and the subjective aspects of the human experience (Nachmias and Nachmias, 1992). As Stake (1995, p.xii) offers, "The qualitative researcher emphasizes episodes of nuance, the sequentiality of happenings in context, the wholeness of the individual."

By working within the SSA as an intern over the period of 1996-1999, I was able to penetrate the surface and immerse myself in the culture of this very complex organization. This led me to develop a research design that would highlight the complexities involved in studying one aspect of an agency. I determined that qualitative methodology would allow the most intimate presentation of the subject matter, without compromising or disturbing the integrity of the organization. It also would provide a foundation for more long-term research activities beyond the scope of this study.

The qualitative techniques chosen, namely internal document analysis, face-to-face interviews, and participant observations, were triangulated to offer a case study of the SSA. Triangulation presents a convergence of data that seem to point in the same direction (Yin, 1993). Qualitative techniques are distinctive in that they take into account the relationship of the researcher to the subject and allow for it to be considered as a natural phenomenon of the methodology.

As Yin states, "The case study has long been stereotyped as a weak sibling among social science methods. Investigators who do case studies are regarded as having deviated from their academic disciplines; their investigations, having insufficient precision, (that is, quantification), objectivity (1989, p.11).

This method may also lend itself in potential bias in the use of evidence (Lipset, Trow, and Coleman, 1962). Typically researchers sift through enormous quantities of detailed information about their cases. In studying contemporary events, a researcher may be the only one to record certain behaviors or phenomena. Certainly the potential for bias is not limited to case studies. One way to counteract the charge is careful documentation using a variety of types and sources of evidence (Johnson and Josylyn, 1986).

However, scholars continue to use the case study method because of its unique ability to contribute to our collective knowledge of individual, organizational, social, and political phenomena. Not surprisingly, the case study has become a common research tool in all the social sciences, allowing an investigator to retain the holistic and meaningful characteristics of real-life events such as individual life cycles, organizational and managerial processes, maturation of bureaucracies, and many other areas (Yin, 1989).

The case study is also used to shed light on the process of implementation. This research may lead to the revision or clarification of existing theories. They may also be the preferred strategy if one wants to learn the details about how something happen and why it may have happened (O'Sullivan and Rassel, 1995). As in all types of research designs, case studies have strengths and weaknesses. In the case of this research study, this type of design best matches the objectives for understanding the implementation of NPR.

Methodology

In the summer of 1997, with the cooperation of my dissertation committee, my research objectives were established. They were:

1. To gather documents that outline the goals that define the services provided by the Southern Region of the Social Security Administration.

2. To gather information on the organizational structure of the Southern Region of the SSA.

3. To gather information on the relationship of the goals to the structure of the Southern Region of the SSA.

4. To gather information on the National Performance Review policy initiative.

5. To gather information on the implementation of the National Performance Review policy initiative in the Southern Region of the SSA.

Collection of Data

These broad objectives served as the central categories into which the information would be sorted. Working within the agency as an intern facilitated my access and authorization to internal documents and key individuals within the organization. Elite interviews of officials were conducted, some of whom allowed me to tape the interviews and others who preferred that I simply take notes. I also observed internal staff meetings, events, and daily operations within the SSA.

Internal Government Documents

The materials can be classified as follows: internal reports, memos, electronic mail, staff notes, correspondence, and General Accounting Office (GAO) reports. Extensive agency and government internal reports are produced to focus on specific areas of the agency, reviewing specific issues facing SSA. SSA produces endless reports on wide ranging subjects, for instance, *Red Book on Work incentives: A Summary guide to Social Security and SSI work incentives with disabilities*, has an internal view of the changes within SSI (SSA, 1995b).

Memos are a key communication link between the different components of the region and captured the flow of information. Electronic mail is a part of the modern communication network and also is collected as a means of discussion between the SSA staff. The regional staff had meetings that discussed internal issues facing the Atlanta region and official notes of these meetings were collected. These note give a detailed perspective on the discussions held within the agency. SSA also has a significant amount of correspondence between different components, agencies, and branches of government.

The GAO, who reviews many government agencies, focused some of their efforts on SSA. For instance in one report, *SSA: Effective Leadership Needed to Meet Daunting Challenge*, GAO investigates the trends and shifts forecast within the agency and the importance of preparing for them (GAO, 1996).

Interviews

The elite interviews were conducted using a flexible but structured method. The individuals used were representatives of a cross section of the central offices, regional offices, congressional staff, and NPR staff. The intent of the interviews was to conceptualize and understand the policy and planning process within SSA and the implementation of NPR. Being in the regional office, I began to set up interviews with the key decision-makers within the regional office. They were chosen on their availability and if they had something to contribute about the implementation of the NPR policy. After a series of these regional meetings I was directed to interview individuals in the Central Offices in Baltimore, more specifically members of the strategic management process and executive staff of the Commissioner of Social Security. My attention then turns to the NPR staff and the Congress.

In the interview process, a basic outline of key points to be discussed was used to keep the interview focused. The questions used sought to understand the evolution of the NPR policy and the way in which this policy was disseminated from the Central Office in Baltimore to the regional offices, specifically the regional office in Atlanta. Information also was gathered on how the policy was implemented and what results were obtained. The questions used are listed in Appendix A. This policy was an executive branch initiative, but many of the proposals required congressional approval, so some key members of Congress and their staff were also interviewed.

The structured interviews maximized the limited time available with each of the individuals interviewed. However, this approach was flexible enough to allow those interviewed to expand on any of the questions if they wished. The interview data was classified according to where the government officials worked, including: a) the Central Office (CO) staff, which encompasses the personnel from Baltimore and Washington, DC, offices; b) the regional office (RO) staff of the southern regional offices in Atlanta, Georgia, and the ten southern states that encompass the southern region; and c) the NPR Staff, based in the Washington, DC, offices.

Development of Propositions

At the beginning of this research project, certain expectations were formulated concerning its probable outcome, including:

1. NPR objectives match the SSA's mission, and can be expeditiously implemented.

2. The effective implementation of NPR in the Southern Region was effective because of the leadership style of a long serving, established Regional Commissioner.

3. The culture within the SSA facilitates the implementation of NPR.

4. That NPR did create organizational change within the Southern Region of SSA.

5. Social Security continually faces changes caused by the shifting demands on the agency.

These expectations warrent further explanation and understanding to why they are vital to the reasoning and to why they were chosen and are further explained as to the first expectation, Social Security always has been focused on sending the right check for the right amount to the right person on time easily fits into the NPR attempt to make "government work better and cost less." By improving customer service and performance, SSA can be used as model for other agencies attempting to deal with the increasing demands from the public.

The second expectation arises because of Gordon Sherman's 24 year hold on the top job of the region. With over 40 year experience with SSA, he understands the dynamics of the organization and is better equipped with the experience to provide leadership for change.

The third expectation, that the culture within the SSA facilitates the implementation of NPR, came about as my experience as an intern within the agency. Most of the individuals who have sought to work in SSA are very dedicated to public service and helping others, which translates into the culture of the agency. For example many of these employees are very active in the community and civic organizations that relate to their daily jobs. The culture of commitment to the public does translate very well into NPR's focus on customer service. The Social Security program is directly helping people economically versus a department of labors where the focus is more abstract.

That NPR did create organizational change within the Southern Region of SSA is because the entire premise of NPR is to make government "work better and cost less" by changing the way in that government operates is the forth expectation. The government is not necessarily filled with bad people but is a bad system with good people in it. Combating this situation would call for drastic organizational change of any government agency trying to implement NPR.

In the previous chapter the major shifts of responsibilities were outlined. This program began with an initial intent and now encompasses a broader mission. SSA also has been constantly under scrutiny to provide world-class service and the increasing demands brought on by the changing demographics. Which leads to the final expectation, that Social Security continually faces changes caused by the shifting demands on the agency can be seen within its evolution.

Testing these expectations provides valuable information regarding their relationship with public administration areas, adds to our understanding of organizational change, and sheds light on how the objectives of the SSA adapt to accommodate the shifting demands of the public. The study examines the import role the leadership plays within the agency at all levels in implementing the NPR policy, and understands the organizational culture and environment within the agency. Finally, the study shows how the NPR policy objectives have been implemented throughout the Southern Region of the SSA.

Conclusions

This study is aimed at discovering how effectively NPR has effected organizational change within the Southern Region of the SSA. This chapter established the theoretical framework and means by which the data collection was organized. Key public administration concepts were addressed to develop an environmental link between implementation and practice. These areas focus on public policy implementation, leadership styles, organizational culture and organizational change. The following two chapters analyzes the data, and the conclusions reached are summarized in chapter seven.

Chapter 6 The Effective Implementation of National Partnership for Reinvention (NPR) within the Social Security Administration (SSA)

The National Performance Review is about change. It will get us moving from red tape to results. It will result in a customer service contract with the American people, one that demonstrates to taxpayers that their tax dollars will be treated with respect for the hard work that earned them.

> Al Gore, Vice President of the United States
> The Rose Garden, The White House, September 7, 1993

This chapter discusses whether and how the National Partnership for Reinvention (NPR) policy was effectively implemented within the southern region of the Social Security Administration (SSA). The focus is on several important aspects of NPR within SSA: how the objectives of NPR compared with the overall mission found within SSA; an analysis of the leadership characteristics used by the Southern Regional Commissioner, Gordon Sherman, in implementing NPR; and a description of some important traits within SSA's organizational culture that influenced the implementation of NPR.

Proposition 1- NPR objectives matched SSA's mission and could be expeditiously implemented.

Implementing the National Partnership for Reinvention (NPR)

The goals developed by NPR were directed toward "reinventing" the entire federal government, while the mission statements for SSA were created to give direction to the agency. NPR's objectives shared common values with SSA's mission statements, thereby facilitating the implementation of NPR. NPR was an ideal policy for SSA. By reviewing and comparing the national objectives of NPR and SSA, NPR influence is assessed in this chapter. In the course of its life, NPR went through several organizational evolutions: reinventing government I (REGO I), REGO II, and REGO III. Each iteration slightly changed NPR's focus. Even though NPR went through several phases, the discussion here considers the initial phase, reinventing government I (REGO I).

Private sector organizations have undergone tremendous changes in the past twenty-five years. These changes were in many ways a reaction to changes in economic markets and the impact of technological improvements. These shifts enabled private sector companies to meet better the demands of the free market. The changes in the private sector did not completely bypass the public sector, and pockets of excellence appeared in nearly every agency inspired by visionary civil servants. In the popular book, *Reinventing Government*, Osborne and Gabler (1993) shared some of the success stories found across the country and the lessons learned from these innovations. There was a tremendous need for change within the federal government and NPR was to be the catalyst that would initiate an active approach to modernizing the federal bureaucracy. NPR was essentially an attempt to improve proactively the public sector.

Within the federal bureaucracy, the Federal Quality Institute was created to focus on promoting the principles of quality management. Within the confines of the federal government there exists a constant tension between two different views: one is concerned with central planning and control, economies of scale, uniformity, and stability, and the other seeks competition, enthusiasm, power of freedom and incentives. Simply put, one side was focused on the process while the other was focused on the outcome (Gore, 1994a, p. 24). This is not a new conflict within government; there has also been a debate over what is the best way to administer government. Most of the previous federal government reform movements had been aimed at improving efficiency.

In 1993, the Clinton administration started out with a great deal of enthusiasm and hope for the ideals and principles embodied in government service. President Clinton was the first baby boomer president and had a personal interest in public policy with a strong commitment to public service. As Clinton began his administration, one of his first major initiatives was to create NPR. By appointing Vice President Gore to head up this task force, he sent an informal signal that NPR was going to be an important initiative. After the creation of this NPR task force, which was composed of an eclectic group of individuals from both inside and outside government, they condensed their objectives into four key principles that focused on change. Each principle would be a hallmark in trying to deal with the mammoth government bureaucracy. These principles were not randomly created ideals, but were based on the collective experience of federal employees. The first phase, REGO I, was aimed at broadening the focus on reform with an emphasis on the best way to service the customer and support the employees.

The first principle was "Cutting Red Tape" (Gore, 1993, p. 11). Red tape refers to the large numbers of rules and regulations confining the authority of federal employees. The regulations stemmed from the reforms of the progressive era and were meant to create more accountability. However, as a result of the excessive regulation, the system had become one in which the focus was more on following the rules than on what was to be accomplished. The paper trail guaranteed accountability.

NPR professed to shift the focus from the process toward the end result. The method selected for doing so was by streamlining budgets, personnel, and procurement systems- thereby liberating organizations to pursue their own missions. By eliminating layers of authority down to the lowest component, the intention was to empower the individuals within government to get the job done (Gore, 1993, p xxxviii).

The second principle was "putting customers first" (Gore, 1993, p. 43). In the private sector, businesses depend on keeping and attracting customers for their continued existence. In government this is not the case. How do they define their customer? Citizens participate in democratic decision making; a customer receives benefits from a specific service. All Americans are citizens, and most are also customers of the post office, Department of Veterans Affairs, and Social Security. All federal agencies should refocus their attention on the needs of these customers (Gore, 1993, p. xxxix), which would lead to eliminating useless actions.

The third principle was "empowering employees to get results" (Gore, 1993, p. 65). Decentralizing authority made it possible for effective entrepreneurial government to flourish. By giving the frontline workers more authority, they would be better able to deal with the issues immediately rather than having to refer every decision up the line to their supervisors, thus preventing stagnation. This allows individuals to feel a part of the system rather than having to fight constantly against it in order to achieve anything (Gore, 1993, p xxxix). Who better to know what works best than the individual who deals directly with the public?

The fourth and final principle was "cutting back to basics: producing better government for less" (Gore, 1993, p. 93). The first step toward producing more for less was to cut the unnecessary layers of regulations. Within the public sector, the trend towards making government work better and cost less demanded a more effective and entrepreneurial approach. By reengineering how they did their work and reexamining programs and processes, public sector workers were able to abandon obsolete practices, eliminate duplication, and end special interest privileges. They invested in greater productivity through loan funds and long-term capital investments, and embraced advanced technologies to cut costs (Gore, 1993, p. xi).

Together, these four principles fit like pieces of a puzzle, coming together as a coherent whole to form a blueprint for the overhaul of the federal government. They did not focus on any particular agency, but attempted to deal with the federal bureaucracy as a whole, in contrast to previous reform efforts that had only focused on limited areas within the federal government. With the support of the executive branch and the Congress, NPR set out to reinvent government and to make it "work better and cost less" (Gore, 1994b, p. 15).

Within the broad outline of these objectives, NPR further spelled out the principles that would put people first: cutting unnecessary spending, serving the government's customers, empowering the government's employees, helping communities to solve their own problems, and fostering excellence. This would be accomplished by creating a clear sense of mission, "steering more and rowing less," delegating authority and responsibility, replacing regulations with incentives, developing budgets based on outcomes, exposing federal operations to competition, searching for market rather than administrative solutions, and measuring NPR's success by customer satisfaction (Gore, 1994c).

Bob Stone, the top career official of NPR, agrees that NPR has had an impact on the way government does business. According to Stone, "Thousands of teams of government workers, many of them with private-public partners, have gotten awards for reinventing government, for doing great things to serve customers or to cut red tape, or to save money. These are people whose lives have been enriched and who have enriched other people's lives" (Government Executive, 1999).

SSA is the largest federal government program, accounting for over one fourth of the federal budget. The agency has been very effective, never missing a payment to a beneficiary and maintaining public confidence (Ball, 2000). These successes have been in large part a result of being able to excel in administering the Social Security programs. As discussed in Chapter 2, increased workloads and diminishing resources led to the evolution of strategic plans within the agency and the creation of mission statements. NPR's contribution was to encourage SSA to reexamine its objectives and vision.

Why is crafting a mission statement so important? The role of a mission statement is to focus on the purpose of an organization, to call attention to what is vital, and to set organizational goals to align practices with values. The exercise of hashing out the fundamental purpose of an organization and debating all the different views held by its members, culminating in the formulation of a basic mission statement, can be very powerful. A well-written mission statement can direct an entire organization from top to bottom. It also helps people at all levels to decide what is a priority.

Before NPR began, the mission statement within SSA was, "to administer national SSA programs as prescribed by legislation, in an equitable, effective, efficient and caring manner" (SSA, 1991, p. 5). This was translated into three goals:

1- To serve the public with compassion, courtesy, consideration, efficiency and accuracy.

2- To protect and maintain the American people's investment in the Social Security Trust funds and to instill public confidence in Social Security programs.

3- To create an environment that ensures a highly skilled, motivated workforce dedicated to meeting the challenges of SSA's public service mission. (SSA, 1991).

Within SSA, the informal or as one official called it the "street" mission is to "get the right check, to the right person, at the right time" (Berkowitz, 1995, p 122) This approach focuses more on getting the work done than what is best for the customer. The business plan listed SSA's core processes as:

enumeration, earnings, claims, post-entitlement, informing the public, and the service delivery interface. These responsibilities are the overt duties that need to be performed.

Since SSA is a federally administered program, it deals with a diverse group of people. SSA has direct contact with the public, either as contributors or beneficiaries. The amount each worker has contributed to the system determines his or her potential benefits, which are calculated using a predetermined formula. This is simple in theory, but the reality is a little more complex. Within the SSA's programs, retirement benefits, disability, and SSI vary in their degree of complexity. The most straightforward is the calculation of retirement benefits, where benefits are determined based on the number of work credits, while there are more stringent calculations and definitions involved in determine disability payments.

With the creation of NPR, SSA was forced to focus on its clientele as customers. In an attempt to adjust to this change, SSA sponsored focus groups within and outside the agency to discover what their customers actually wanted. Concurrently, the Government Results and Performance Act of 1993 (GPRA) required the agency to have a mission statement with objectives linked to performance measures (GAO, 1997a). GPRA was not part of NPR, but did share similar ideas of making agencies work better. The requirements of GPRA stated that all agencies needed to have written business plans and yearly accountability reports, thus creating a way to rate the performance of government (Marshall, 1997).

The strategic plan was produced by executives and endorsed by all parts of the agency, led by a strategic management office based in the SSA's central offices. Other groups providing input to the strategic plan were: SSA employees, SSA managers, citizens, congressional committees, the White House, the Office of Management and Budget, other levels of government, interest groups, other agencies and departments (Gracie, 1997). This plan went through an intensive process to determine the focus of the agency. In the final draft, NPR's influence was apparent, with a clear focus on the customer and staff.

As spelled out in the agency's strategic plan, the long-term goals of the SSA are:

1. Responsive programs: to promote valued, strong, and responsive Social Security programs and conduct effective policy development, research, and program evaluation;

2. World-class service: to deliver customer-responsive, world-class service;

3. Program management: to make Social Security Administration program management the best in the business, with zero tolerance for fraud and abuse;

4. Value employees: to be an employer that values and invests in each employee; and

5. To strengthen public understanding of the Social Security program

(SSA, 1995, p.4).

As part of the process of achieving these long-term goals, the agency formulated three short-term goals:

1. To rebuild confidence in Social Security;

2. To provide world-class service; and

3. To create a supportive environment for employees (SSA, 1995c).

It is these three short-term goals that are most commonly referred to by the organization's leadership. The objective of a business plan is to explain to outsiders what an organization does and to give a vision to those working within the organization. One high level official illustrated her vision of this mission statement with a story from National Aeronautical and Space Administration (NASA). During the height of the space race, a janitor was asked what he did at NASA. He replied simply, "I am helping put a man on the moon" (Sherin-Jones, 1997). Similarly, SSA employees should feel a part of the organization and that they contribute to its overall goal. Unfortunately, because of the complexity and sheer size of the organization, there are pockets of employees who lack this sense of connection (Sherin-Jones, 1997).

These goals were meant to shape policy and enable the agency to focus on what is important. However, there were no direct tangible measures of the effectiveness in these areas. One executive staff member summed up the strategic goals by concluding that there was no direct link between the national level and the local field office. SSA does not have a simple cause and effect model. The "number crunchers" cannot say with accuracy that a particular local district office is responsible for 1/1600 of the national objective. Many of the SSA initiatives overlap and move in similar directions. SSA is very good at administering the programs, but not very effective in increasing efficiency (Gracie, 1997). Others commented that there was a "need for less checkers and more doers. The system has not changed since the 1970s and what is expected becomes a self-fulfilling prophecy" (Sherman, 1996). SSA's goals are entirely operational: its work is readily observable and its outputs are easily and fully measurable.

In internal communications, there was a push toward improving the strategic management process. The following memo focuses on the idea of quality underlying the purpose:

> We must create specific objectives that will lead to long-term improvements that are tied to the organization goals and mission. The goals must be clearly defined; expected accomplishments should be identified that will produce measurable results that are directly related to improving services. A monitoring service must also be in place to track these customer driven initiatives and measure the strategic effectiveness of each. Finally, these initiatives must be clearly communicated to all levels of the organization to the point that each employee can articulate the goals, understand and be accountable for his/her role in the success of the endeavor (Warden, 1997).

Another internal workgroup developed ideas and recommendations that focused on where work could best be handled, given staffing imbalances, the operational environment and expectations of further systems support. Recommendations from the workgroup included:

- Work should be performed close to the point of delivery.

- Support functions should be provided as close as possible to the "front line"

- SSA must continue to provide public contact facilities for the foreseeable future, but must also have the capability of dealing the work in a centralized manner.

- The options for delivering service would continue to be face to face, mail, and telephone.

- Continued systems enhancements (Oasis, 1997a)

The workgroup looked at whether SSA should provide a service through a centralized or localized approach, concentrating on the best method to deliver that service most efficiently. Production is rapidly being replaced by performance. Even though SSA is not in the business of retaining the patronage of their

clients, the agency realized that the service component is becoming more important in the public sector.

The agency needed to examine the key factors that govern service quality and build the framework for

managing and providing that service. In constructing a strategic plan, SSA concluded that it was necessary

to blend operational imperatives and service strategies (Harmon, 1997).

Compare and Contrast NPR and SSA

From earlier discussion in the chapter the principles of NPR, SSA appears to be the ideal agency to

implement this reform policy. From these two sets of goals, SSA took the lead in working with the NPR

task force to ensure that SSA became a change organization, better able to meet its responsibilities.

Over the years, there have been many governmental reform movements, but NPR was different.

The core NPR staff was made up of a combination of Vice President Gore's staff, political appointees and

detailees, and federal employees on temporary assignment to the NPR staff, and operated under the

jurisdiction of the executive branch. The NPR budget comes from a combination of different agencies but

the initiative was informally part of the executive branch staff. Their NPR central office location was

directly across from the White House. This organizational structure created an environment that was

designed to facilitate creativity without managerial order. The top career civil servant, Bob Stone, was given

the title of "energizer in chief." When visiting the NPR offices, this lack of organization created an

impression of chaos that perhaps not coincidentally could best be described as resembling the headquarters

of a political campaign. Cramped spaces, papers everywhere and people coming and going all the time were

the norm. This was both a benefit and drawback to the program's success.

NPR was broadly focused on reforming the entire federal government. However, some federal

agencies were more open to NPR than others; this was the case for SSA. In interviews with the NPR staff,

they already perceived themselves as change agents. NPR's informal agenda was to plant the seeds of

change that would eventually evolve into a revolutionary shift within the federal government. The NPR

staff initially sought to point out the deficiencies of the federal structure and attempt to correct them using innovative approaches. "We are change agents and will transform the federal government into a lean and efficient machine", stated Tom Flavin, NPR staff member. The NPR staff believed that it was not that people in government were bad, indeed quite the opposite, but that they were good people locked in a bad system (Flavin, 1997). The staff's efforts were expected to change the public's opinion of government. No longer would the phrase, "I am from the government and am here to help you" be seen as a bad joke (Kane, 1997). In my visits to the NPR main office, there was a high energy level among staffers that could best be described as a cult-type culture.

When speaking to the officials at SSA, it was clear that several factors had led to their ready embrace of NPR. First of all, there was the huge emphasis and high level of public attention focused on NPR by the administration. Secondly, Clinton's new Commissioner, Shirley Chater, was deeply committed to NPR's success within SSA. Finally, SSA's track record of good customer service ideally matched NPR's goals (Carter, 1997).

Interviews with the NPR staff revealed that the initial intent of NPR was to garner momentum and support for this task force. They achieved a positive image by creating a high level of publicity focusing on the policy's potential. By reaching out to the talent already available within the federal government and benchmarking with other organizations, NPR was able to foster cooperation within the federal community. Willett Bunton (1998) expressed her experience being a NPR staff member. "When Al Gore came to the Defense department for a town hall meeting, I stood up and openly shared my ideas about improving my job. To my surprise, not only were my ideas welcomed, but I was asked to become a part of NPR. Now I am making a difference in changing the federal government." As President Clinton declared at the inception of NPR, "the federal government is broken and we intend to fix it" (Clinton, 1993).

The NPR staff implemented over 90% of the proposals made in its first report. Based on the recommendations in this report, President Clinton signed over 22 directives, over 100 agencies published customer service standards, nine agencies started major streamlining initiatives, many agencies formed labor-management partnerships with their unions, and 135 "reinvention laboratories" throughout the federal government were set up to foster innovation (GAO, 1996d).

The first step in formalizing this process of reinventing government occurred in September 1994, when NPR published its first status report, setting out the changes that were underway and making over 384 recommendations. The federal employees who worked on the teams went back to their home agencies to carry out the reinvention initiatives and help define and develop standards (Gore, 1994b).

As a result of executive orders and presidential directives, NPR was a priority for all executive departments. This top-down approach was designed to direct agencies to take action and focus on implementing NPR. Across the country, workshops were held to discuss NPR and the benefits of this new policy. In 1994, Georgia State University sponsored a one-day workshop on NPR that covered all the basics. The director of NPR, Bob Stone, expressed a view held by many when he stated that the "public sector needs to reform the way government functions and follow a similar path to that found in the private sector" (Stone, 1994).

At the same conference, Alice Rivlin, Deputy Director of the Office of Management and Budget, pointed to the reasons why NPR should be effective, saying "the administration is pushing for reform, the requirements of the GPRA legislation, a decade of private sector change and that the federal government is broken" (Rivlin, 1994).

The conference in Atlanta was the first in the South addressing the challenges and opportunities brought about by NPR. The attendees included members of the federal community in Atlanta and it was an attempt to sell NPR to the upper levels of administration of the regional offices. This effort ideally would energize the federal workers to spread the news of a movement that would filter down to the lower channels. This broad coalition of federal employees from within different agencies would use the objectives of NPR to help their agencies move into the next phase of reinventing government.

According to interviews, the NPR staff's view was that these simple objectives would translate into action in a short time because the individuals who wrote the objectives were already part of the federal community. They had a stake in NPR's success and would go back to their home agencies and spread the gospel of NPR's virtues. Their credibility was that they would not be a group of biased outsiders who sided with the politically charged rhetoric; rather they were committed public servants who wanted to mend what was wrong and make government better. When talking to NPR staff, both in Washington and throughout the country, they all seemed to have an enthusiasm for the potential of NPR. These individuals felt that they were in a position to change the operation of government for the better. These enthusiastic team players traveled the country speaking on the objectives and short-term successes of NPR. This enthusiasm would transmit optimism for change with the aid of this policy, positively impacting the federal community. These change agents were ready to challenge the old ways of doing business; to them, NPR was more than a policy, it was a way of life.

SSA used NPR as a catalyst for change and benefited from the policy window created by this new policy. Commissioner Chater saw NPR as an opportunity to gain access to the White House by aligning herself with one of the administration's principal policy objectives (Chater, 1996). In making NPR succeed, it would give the commissioner needed political capital and support for her own initiatives within the agency. As seen in the earlier review of the history of SSA, every commissioner seeks to leave a long lasting imprint and implement useful change within the agency.

Chater was in a tough position at SSA because she was not the first choice of the administration and SSA is a very politically-charged organization. She was caught between the administration and the bureaucracy and had to balance both to get anything accomplished during her tenure. Chater prioritized NPR by creating an executive-level staff position that specifically focused on NPR and its implementation across the agency. The role of this person was to act as a liaison between the NPR staff and SSA. The NPR staff was anxious to have concrete evidence that they were making government work better and cost less and they were pleased to discover that SSA was willing to be their test case.

At a management conference in 1994, Chater spoke about the need to deal with constant change. The theme of her talk was "The Future of SSA." The agency was facing some tension in dealing with this significant change. Some of the major changes were the transition into an independent agency, health care reform, and welfare reform. By being able to do things smarter and differently from the old way, SSA would be in a better position to openly discuss the differences apparent to the leadership. Over 2,500 employees participated in discussion groups and shared insights into what the agency needed. The management team in the Central Offices in Baltimore acted as the "central facilitator," emphasizing teamwork, partnership, and focus on customer service. By being able to "put the customer first," the agency would be in a better position to meet the challenges facing the agency. By executive order, NPR had already come to influence the way in which the agency did business. The close relationship between NPR and SSA was apparent. Among the goals of SSA, there is a direct correlation between what has been stated and what is expected.

The first goal, *to improve public confidence* (SSA,1995c) is directly addressed by making sure that there is accountability for the agency's actions, by the agency becoming pro-active and sharing the facts, by ensuring that the benefits will be there for all working Americans, and by making sure that SSA does not add to the deficit and that there are enough benefits to continue making payments to beneficiaries until 2029. The second goal, *world-class service* (SSA, 1995c) would take a commitment from all the agency's employees. Dr. Chater cited a study reporting that one-half of all the taxes collected were lost to waste and one-half of what the government did needed to change. Her tenure would focus on staying ahead of the process and changing the workplace. Over the next two years she planned a 15% reduction in staff, with more of the remaining people being moved to the front lines (Chater, 1994).

The transformation of SSA from being under health and human services (HHS) toward independent agency status will make the agency more visible. With looming health care reforms, the agency will need to prepare for increased responsibilities (Chater, 1994).

NPR did allow Dr. Chater to have better access to the administration and be actively involved in dealing with some problems within SSA. One area in particular was handling the increasingly complex disability review area. An incredible backlog had built up and she commissioned studies and attempted to redesign the program in a way that would improve adjudication of the claims. Under Dr. Chater's leadership, the focus on redefining the role of the customer was an important shift. Instead of reacting to what the customer wanted, the agency would act on what was best for the customer.

However, other factors contributed to limiting the effective implementation of NPR during Dr. Chater's term. SSA became an independent agency and had to focus its attention on redefining its role and seeking its new identity. The political climate created from the turmoil of becoming an independent agency, prevented her from being confirmed as Commissioner for the new independent agency and she had to leave. She was followed by a series of other commissioners whose tenure was so short that any dramatic imprint was not apparent.

SSA has always been focused on meeting the demands of the public and its staff processes all the checks, provides the benefits and administers all the programs under the SSA's umbrella. One area in which NPR influenced the agency was in making SSA specifically focus on its clientele as "the customer," not just an anonymous beneficiary, using the private sector's usual catchphrase, "the customer is always right."

The focus on the customer became apparent when President Clinton signed an Executive Order formalizing customer service standards. This required that all executive departments and agencies publish a customer service plan by September 8, 1994 that could be understood by their customers. The executive order defines the customer as the "individual or entity who is directly served by a department or agency." The executive order defines what actions are to be taken and formalized the process (Executive Order No 12862, 1993).

The focus on the customer was the central focus of the administration. For instance, in a memo from the White House about NPR, the clear focus was on improving customer service. All executive departments and agencies were required to identify and survey their customers and establish customer service standards to guide the operations of the executive branch. By September 1, 1995, the results were to be published and available to the public. The agencies needed an ongoing basis with which to measure the results achieved compared to normal customer service standards and report them annually. These measures were to be linked to the GPRA requirements and be aligned with a customer focus. Within each agency, employees were to be surveyed on ideas to improve customer service and actions were to be taken to motivate them. As the memo states, "without satisfied employees, we cannot have satisfied customers. Agencies should also initiate consolidation of services across jurisdictions and develop a one stop shop approach" (Clinton, 1995).

When speaking to officials from the commissioner's staff, they pointed out that although this focus on the customer was not necessarily new, it was a shift in the way SSA did business. The survey that was conducted internally and externally was able to define what the agency needed to improve on and what exactly the public demanded. SSA's office of policy conducts several evaluative research studies annually on SSA's programs (Lelane, 1997).

Prior to NPR, the way the agency dealt with the public had been the same for years: if someone needed an SSA benefit, they went to the local office, took a number, and waited until they were called. The customer survey told a different story, revealing that the public wanted either to be able to call and solve a problem over the phone or, for more complex issues, set up an appointment to meet someone with the authority to solve the problem. The public also advocated using modern technological capabilities to meet their needs, i.e. the Internet. One priority thus became the 800 number telephone service.

At an SSA managerial conference in Atlanta, Georgia on August 10, 1994, Dr. Lawrence Thompson, Deputy Commissioner of SSA, related how NPR was an integral part of SSA objectives. Thompson argued,

What NPR did was to help government shift its paradigm and increase employee empowerment, flatten the bureaucratic structure, and streamline the process. One example used was what customer service meant to each employee. How do you define this? Well, first of all, what is it that SSA customers, the American People, want from the agency? Customer Service surveys show that Americans want more of a one shop stopping approach to government, rather than a tiered hierarchical system. This can be achieved by allowing each person within the agency to take a proactive approach (Thompson, 1994).

Citing an internal *Best Practices on Customer Service* report, he shared some examples of reforming the reception area, conducting outreach, and better use of the 800 service (Thompson, 1994). SSA's commitment to meeting Executive Order 12862 will not end with the publication of its customer service plan and standards. Thomson stressed this priority, saying "We are committed to taking the actions that will allow us to achieve each standard and to continue listening to customers and employees to find out what we need to provide world class service" (Thompson, 1994). Overall, the existing mission and similarity to NPR facilitated implementation within SSA. Many SSA employees actively embraced the changes brought in by NPR. As Joe Thompson, a staff member from the New York regional office, stated in the internal SSA magazine, *Oasis*,

> All organizations and institutions in society are undergoing tremendous pressures to transform themselves. People can't just show up for work and follow the old rules without questioning, updating, revising, and changing them to suit new and different requirements. Organizations must be flexible and capable of change or they will atrophy or die. Employees must be both innovative and creative in doing their jobs effectively" (Thompson, 1996, p 8).

As shown by the comments of the SSA staff, the redefinition of the customer was one of the most important changes that was brought about by NPR. Agency staff had always been very aware of the needs of the customer, but they had never before taken the time to listen to what their customers were saying. The customers were asking for more personalized attention and a simplification of the process used to process their claims. In one particular executive staff meeting, there was a long discussion on how "customer service" needed to be adjusted to this end. Those attending the meeting concluded that the agency needed to improve phone request time and also the scheduling of appointments in the field (Harmon, 1997c). SSA's top priorities continued to include: world class service, the 800 number, a supportive work environment, and restoring the public's confidence in the agency (Harmon, 1997a).

SSA is strongly committed to discipline, and accurate assessment of all aspects of its performance. In addition, because of the scope and impact of SSA's programs on American society as a whole, SSA is closely monitored by GAO and OIG, and frequently receives input from them where SSA lacks sufficient evaluative information (Oasis, 1996). The agency's six performance areas are as follows: current program outcomes; responsible operations; effective program information; world class service; efficient administration; and supportive employee environment.

The mission of the agency tends to lean more toward abstract, "feel good" goals. However, the agency has a history of keeping track of its responsibilities. For each strategic objective, performance indicators and target performance levels were developed by the intercomponent team responsible for preparing the Program for Objective Achievement. This highly participatory process brought objectivity to the formulation of performance indicators and targets. Some examples of outcome measures used for mission-critical activities include: the percentage of initial SSI aged claims processed within 14 days of filing; the percentage of social security cards issued within 5 days of receiving all necessary documentation; the percentage of 800 number callers assisted within 5 days of receiving all necessary documentation; the percentage of the public perceiving SSA service to be good, very good or excellent; the percentage of OASI payment outlays without overpayments; and the percentage of increase of debt collected.

These different objectives and activities of the agency are part of its normal administrative responsibility. It is thus difficult to tell if the NPR objectives were created to fit SSA's activities or if SSA's strategic goals were realigned to fit the NPR model, but regardless of the underlying change mechanism, the end result was positive.

Proposition 2-The implementation of NPR in the Southern Region was effective because of the leadership style of a long serving, established Regional Commissioner

What makes the Southern region unique is that of the ten regions that comprise the SSA structure, it is the largest and most diverse. The region has always outperformed other regions and is often showcased as an example of excellence in government. One reason why the implementation of NPR in the Southern

Region was effective was because of the leadership and longevity of the regional commissioner, Gordon Sherman. Three leadership characteristics Gordon Sherman possesses that were vital to NPR success were his skills as a visionary, his emotional intelligence, and his policy entrepreneurship.

Defining leadership

As defined by Denhardt, effective leadership is "The character of the relationship between the individual and a group or organization that stimulates or releases some latent energy or organization within the group so that those involved more clearly understand their own needs, desires, interest, and potentialities and begin to work toward their fulfillment" (Denhardt 1981, p. x). The leadership skills needed by public leaders, therefore, are not the skills of management or manipulation commonly seen in commercial organizations, but rather the skills required to assist individuals and groups in realizing their fullest potential. Leadership, in this view, is educative and concerned primarily with human growth and development.

Role of the Regional Commissioner

The job description of the regional commissioner outlines responsibilities for general supervision, coordination and management of all Social Security activities and programs in the eight Southeastern States. This responsibility encompasses the provision of social security service to the 35 million plus citizens of this area via more than 300 districts field offices facilities staffed with over 10,000 federal employees, 9 state disability agencies on contract with approximately 2000 employees. This includes issuing cash payments of approximately $20 billion every year.

Gordon Sherman's Background

Gordon Sherman has been with SSA for over forty years, of which twenty-two years have been as regional commissioner. He holds a law degree from Woodrow Wilson College of Law from John Marshall University and received his undergraduate degree from Auburn University. He began his career as a claims representative in Anniston, Alabama on November 24, 1958. He was promoted to the Atlanta Regional office in October 1960 and progressed through administrative and staff positions to Assistant Regional

Commissioner in 1969. He was appointed regional commissioner in 1975. President Carter appointed him to the Senior Executive Service in 1979.

During his service with Social Security, he has received several prestigious awards, including one from the National Academy of Public Administrators in 1990 recognizing him as an outstanding public administrator, of which he was elected a fellow in 1992, and was awarded the meritorious Presidential Rank Award in 1998 by President Clinton, the highest honor a civil servant can receive.

Gordon Sherman also has a strong commitment to public service. Through this commitment, I had the opportunity to get to know him. He sponsors a lecture series at Auburn University's Maters of Public Administration program with the objective of bringing practicing public administrators on campus to share their insights into how government operates on a personal level. At one of these seminars, I met Mr. Sherman and he sparked my interest in SSA and agreed to provide me with the access I needed to perform this research.

SSA is a hierarchical organization. The central offices in Baltimore include the commissioner's office and many of the Senior Executive Service (SES) leadership offices. The regional offices oversee the state directors and they in turn oversee district offices. The tele-service centers and the State Disability Determination Services (DDS) report directly to Baltimore. What makes the southern region unique is that the regional commissioner overseeing this region has remained in post for longer than the commissioner of any other region. This has had both a positive and a negative impact on the way the region functions.

Gordon Sherman's Leadership Characteristics

Gordon Sherman's years as regional commissioner have been some of the most turbulent in the agency's history. The agency was transformed from a board to a sub-cabinet office and then into an independent agency during his tenure. SSA has also become more political due to both the increase in the number of political appointees at the top levels of the agency and the higher priority it was given within the national agenda by political leaders responding to the changes created by shifting demographics. Sherman is unique in the SSA organization; he has the longest tenure as regional commissioner and was promoted from the lowest levels of the organization.

In his notes for a speech given to Southeastern Federal Recruiting Personnel Conference, Sherman outlined his perspective on the role of leadership. He considers that regardless of the size or scope of an organization, leadership makes the primary difference in all successful organizations. In his view, there is a direct correlation between good leadership and good management. The phrases that link the two most effectively are "managers do things right" and "leaders do the right things." Managers tend to look at situations more from the control point of view, a by-the-book and numbers approach, which often stymies creativity, imagination and teamwork. Such an attitude can easily lead to an overly bureaucratic organization, where employees do not feel good about themselves and their work activities. He goes on to say:

> In today's society/culture, leadership is more important than managerial or technical operations. While I do not downplay the need for both managerial and technical expertise, leadership is more important and required at all levels- not only at the top, but also throughout the organization. Many of the problems in most organizations at all levels today are not technical or managerial, but problems of leadership. Leaders cannot, and do not, sit around and wait for someone to tell them what to do, or what they want, or wait for their supervisors to do their thing. A leader will step out and be creative, imaginative, and say to others, "Follow Me!" Therefore, this moves the unit to an objective down the road, versus just concentrating on today's issues and problems.

> But, in order to lead, there are certain principles practiced by all leaders, at any level, or any individual style he or she may have. These are commitment, vision, inspiration, continual learning, and accountability (Sherman, 1999).

Understanding Sherman's view on leadership makes it possible to identify several of the qualities that facilitated the implementation of NPR. These qualities can be grouped into three leadership characteristics that Sherman espouses. These include being a visionary, an emotional but intelligent leader, and a policy entrepreneur. He explained, "[It is necessary to] create within the group environment a good attitude, and teams need to develop themselves. There must be a vision of where you want to go and you must serve as an example" (Sherman, 1998).

Visionary

The consensus reached in the literature on of management styles is that effective leaders within organizations often are visionaries. This enables the organization to have someone who gives direction and conveys an understanding as to what is expected and needed for the organization to produce results. Sherman's vision was aimed at making the Southern Region the best performing region in SSA. He accomplished this by choosing competent personnel and encouraging innovation. This was already part of his style before the inception of NPR. Sherman expressed vision as being, "The leader knows where he/she is going, unwavering. There is no question where he/she wants to be - the driving force" (Sherman, 1999). The objective that was repeated over and over again within staff meetings was to work on making Atlanta the best performing region and this approach has succeeded, making the Atlanta region the most productive and efficient within the entire agency. This can be credited to Sherman's leadership style of constantly seeking ways to improve methods of completing the increased workloads at the SSA.

To hear him tell it, Sherman leadership style is quite simple. To develop an environment that will foster the best performance from the individuals in any organization, it is important to empower individuals and help them help themselves, and allow individuals the space and innovation to tackle their responsibilities and find methods to accomplish the ever increasing workloads.

Sherman's management style is that of the classical chief executive officer (CEO), where he is the figurehead of the southern region and makes all major decisions. His deputy is responsible for the day-to-day decisions, while Sherman represents the leadership and promotes the agency within the region. This approach is coupled with an active pursuit of networking with other executives that is not simply limited to the public sector. During his tenure at SSA, he has also served on several bank and community boards and is actively involved within the Atlanta community. He is a master networker with the skill to bring diverse groups together to find a common ground and mediate solutions that create an amicable consensus.

Observing his management style during private staff meetings, Gordon Sherman constantly works to eliminate the bureaucracy and open the lines of communication. The focus is on the results and holding departments and individuals accountable for assigned tasks. "The Regional Commissioner indicated to us that he felt the entire region staff was responsible for goal achievement. He specifically mentioned he felt the program staffs were unaccountable for performance in their areas of responsibility" (SSA, 1998e). In the staff notes compilation, after a review of the state of the region was discussed, specific action items were assigned to different members of the staff. A common phrase repeated was that "An organization does well what the boss checks." Sherman constantly stated, "You can never get rid of the human aspect of the organization."

His forty plus years of working for SSA give Gordon Sherman an extensive institutional knowledge from which to work. He is referred to as the dean of the regional commissioners and this grants him a little more versatility in being innovative within the overall program. The region has often been chosen to create pilot programs that are eventually replicated by other regions.

Emotional Intelligence (EQ)

Emotional Intelligence best describes the approach taken by Sherman in dealing with his staff and the organization in the Southern Region. Daniel Goleman (1998) wrote about the EQ- emotional intelligence. A person's EQ is his capacity to relate to both him/herself and others. Goleman argues that there are five components to a person's emotional intelligence. Three of these components measure an individual's relationship to themself: self-awareness, self-regulation, and personal motivation. The other two components are empathy for others and social skills, both measuring one's relationships with others. To gain a place on the corporate ladder, one needs reasonable intelligence and technical competencies.

However, as one climbs up the chain, the qualities of leadership include a good mind and a strong emotional intelligence. Goleman writes,

> The higher the rank of a person considered to be a star performer, the more emotional intelligence capability showed up as the reason for his or her effectiveness. When I compare star performers with average performers in senior leadership positions, nearly 90 percent of the difference in their profiles was attributed to EQ factors rather than cognitive abilities (Goleman, 1998, p 199).

EQ is a good way to describe Gordon Sherman's ability to connect with his staff and inspire loyalty and respect. This has been an essential skill that has enabled him to move up quickly through the ranks within SSA and allowed him to enjoy a long tenure within the agency. This openness has also been a means by which Gordon Sherman learns new ideas and seeks input from his staff. Because identifying future leaders is a key element in any organization's success, he has mentored many individuals. Throughout the agency, you can see the imprints of the active mentoring that Gordon Sherman has undertaken. He actively seeks individuals with potential and empowers them to succeed. He even enjoys saying how many of his supervisors in Baltimore were once under his leadership and have now moved up to oversee him.

One key feature within SSA's culture is its rich history and the way it acknowledges achievement through ceremonial and ritual activity. I observed several examples of this activity that had an important impact on the successes of individuals. A case in point was the installation of a manager within a district office. Gordon Sherman personally oversaw the ceremony and administered the oath of office to the district manager, in which the new manager vowed to continue his commitment to public service. In an interview after the ceremony, he stated that this was a very important ritual because we are a society filled with rituals, graduations, weddings, and parties. An installation ceremony for a new district manager not only recognizes their accomplishments, but also makes their actions accountable to their family, friends, and the community. This often produces better district managers and benefits the agency.

This can also be observed at regional management conferences. Each of these conferences is about more than simply conveying ideas and bringing the management staff up to date on the state of the agency;

it is also used to recognize achievement and for networking. The participants are usually compensated for travel and expenses and allowed to enjoy a small perk of the job. These conferences are also a means for the field staff to interact with the regional staff, giving them a chance to identify future leaders within the region.

Every two years there is a diversity conference sponsored by the SSA's central office. This conference is aimed at emphasizing diversity and its importance within and outside the agency. SSA's clientele is very diverse and the agency strives to have the people working within SSA reflect the people they serve. The aging of the agency has forced many of the senior members of the agency to consider how they will develop human capital for the future. By mentoring and developing positive relationships, they intend to improve the future of administration.

Policy Entrepreneur

As Kingdon (1994) describes it, effective leaders in the public sector are policy entrepreneurs. They are not held back by the bureaucratic limitations, but seek windows of opportunity to create change and implement policies directed by them. In the case of NPR, Sherman did several things that facilitated its effective implementation. First, he created a point person on his executive staff to head up the operations. Sherman also developed a personal relationship with Linda Walker, the Southern representative of NPR, who herself had a close personal relationship with Vice President Gore, thus facilitating communications with NPR.

Gordon Sherman's tenure has been filled with examples of how he initiated new ideas that became part of the overall agency's operational method. One of Sherman's first actions as Regional Commissioner was to create the Regional Commissioner Inquiry Unit (RCIU). This unit was the first in the nation to handle concerns from congressional offices. This reduced one level of bureaucracy and created a point of contact for congressional staffers attempting to help a constituent with a problem concerning SSA (Sherman, 1997).

By being an assiduous networker, he has been able to convey insights between the worlds of business, academia, and government. This was one reason why NPR appealed to his style, and he has been a strong advocate for its success within the southern region. He regularly takes on new responsibilities as part of his civic duty. For example, in reaching out to the federal community, Sherman, who was at the time the chair of the Federal Executive Board, led over 1,200 federal employees loaned to the 1996 Olympic committee to help with the security detail. The federal employees functioned as the eyes and ears of the security detail and became an integral part of the success of the Atlanta Olympics.

His successes with NPR were part of his being a policy entrepreneur. One example of how this was effective was the Georgia Common Access Program, touted as a success by NPR in countless reports and presentations. This project was an ideal fit with the NPR role of reinventing government. What it sought to do was to bring forth a common access framework for both state and federal agencies. In theory, why would a person who needed some government service have to go to the state and then to a federal agency and fill out essentially identical application forms? With modern electronic data transfer capabilities, the same information should not have to be given twice.

As quoted in the executive summary, "Georgia Common Access (GCA) grew out of former President Carter's call for a simpler application process in response to needs expressed by the Atlanta project communities and with the support of the Federal Executive Board." A project workgroup was organized who took on the task of merging 64 pages of individual applications into a "seamless" eight page, multi-program GCA application that was tested in Atlanta by the U.S. Department of Agriculture Food and Consumer Service, the Department of Housing and Urban Development, the Georgia Department of Human Resources, the Department of Health and Human Services Administration for Children and Families, Health Care Financing Administration, and the Social Security Administration.

In a personal handwritten note to Vice President Gore, President Carter touting the success of the program and the need for the administration to take note, wrote, "Under reinventing government, this should be done nationwide. We are eager to help with Congress and the states, with your leadership" (Carter, 1994). Gore responded to Carter, "Congratulations on this historic accomplishment. Your leadership has led to a critical step in the reinvention of the welfare of bureaucracy" (Gore, 1993). He further stated that his staff was aware of the success of the Atlanta project and that the NPR staff was going to promote it nationwide and urge other Federal Executive Boards to take on a similar initiative. This project received a "Hammer" award for its innovation and has been used as an example of how government is changing the way in which government does its business.

SSA took the lead in developing a "one-stop-shop" in Atlanta, Georgia. During my internship in the agency, I was designated as Sherman's representative and attended several meetings to discuss the introduction of this project. The administration's intent was to centralize several offices into one location so that anyone could go in and obtain access to government services in a "one-stop" location, like a general store. The public had asked for the creation of a service like this that would be specifically designed to enable them to get the services they needed immediately.

In background information, Sherman revealed that this was an idea he had supported for years. However, dealing with the bureaucracy and bringing all these varying agencies together was complex. The initial obstacle was funding and staffing. Each related agency would be required to commit a certain amount of funds to the project in order to make the one-stop-shop sustainable. This did occur to a certain extent, but some agencies could not come up with adequate funding in time for the opening so SSA took the lead by funding a substantial part of the project.

The opening day was set for June 20, 1996. Several dignitaries were present for the opening, including the local Congressman John Lewis, Mayor Bill Campbell, and the U.S. Commissioner of SSA, Shirley Chater. Vice President Gore did not attend the event but sent an email stating "it just makes good common sense to locate as many government services as possible right here in one place. In Atlanta's new U.S. General Store, this is the very type of one-stop-shopping and customer-friendly service that people have come to expect and there is no reason our government can't provide the same. Congratulations and keep up the good work!!" (Gore, 1996).

The U.S. General Store has representatives from over 14 different state and federal agencies. The layout of the General Store has desks for specialized assistance, kiosks for electronic information, and personal computers for Internet access. The services available at this location are not limited to the physical office but are also offered on the web, opening up a window for web users to gain access to the information provided by these government agencies.

A "Hammer Award" ceremony that I attended on September 13, 1996 was a recognition of the Tennessee electronic access project. This project was similar to the Common Access Project in Georgia. It had been operational for over two years and provided 30 SSA field offices in Tennessee with on-line real time access to select state data. The information available deals with vital statistics (such as births, deaths, marriages, and divorces); wage data; Medicaid; motor vehicles; food stamps; unemployment compensation, etc. The results of this project took SSA one step closer to its goal of achieving world-class service by reducing the shuffle of clients between state agencies and SSA field offices. General Accounting Office estimates that if the Tennessee access project were expanded nationally, it would result in a saving to SSA of an estimated $89.3 million in overpayments made because SSA did not have current state information. As a direct result of SSA having on-line access to state data, the state has requested reciprocal on-line access to SSA data. This process is being developed and will be piloted in Tennessee.

In visiting local field offices (FO), this attempt to consolidate information revealed the advantages of the ready transfer of information and was another way for the agency to make government "work better and cost less." There are always ceremonies for recognition of outstanding employees as a means to showcase excellence. As quoted on the program for one such event,

> The regional commissioner award is presented to employees in recognition of outstanding service to the SSA. You have demonstrated extraordinary dedication in using your abilities to accomplish the objectives of SSA and are deserving of recognition. We recognize you as dedicated individuals who have represented the Atlanta Region well. Your exceptional achievements serve as a good example for others to follow (SSA, 1996).

After observing the interaction between the staffs of NPR and the Southern Region, it became clear that there was another indirect relationship that enabled NPR to assume a prominent role: the Southern

Director for NPR was a former district office director for Vice President Gore when he was the Senator from Tennessee. This indirect link gave a clearer connection with the Vice President and his staff. Even within the ranks of the civil service, access to political influence can build needed political capital for bureaucrats who are trying to influence the larger bureaucracy and shape effective policy.

Proposition 3- The Culture within the SSA facilitated the implementation of NPR

NPR was expected to change dramatically the business of government. It was going to transform it from a highly centralized bureaucracy into a lean, flat, and learning organization. Most of the broad objectives sought by NPR were visible within SSA, but the agency was a large, complex organization with a history of success. The question was asked -- what would be gained by satisfying the latest political craze, NPR?

Brief review of culture

SSA is a large organization and within it there are many layers. Within each of these exists a distinct set of cultural characteristics that influence the way the program is administered (Derthick, 1979). These cultures also facilitated the implementation of NPR. This section examines some broad characteristics that capture the culture of SSA as a whole, along with those that specifically apply to the Southern Region. All are characteristics that have a direct impact on the implementation of NPR. Applying Schein's (1985) level of culture model to SSA shows how some traits within SSA facilitated the implementation of NPR.

As defined, culture can be described as the "personality" of the organization. By being immersed within the agency as an intern, I was in a good position to understand the culture and determine which characteristics facilitated the implementation of NPR within SSA. I experienced firsthand the stories, artifacts, and life found within this large bureaucracy. The size and complexity of the organization prevents anyone from fully experiencing all the cultural characteristics found within this agency. However, within regions, states and departments, certain characteristics reflect a broader view of the overall culture.

Organizational culture literature has grown out of a disenchantment with the way organizational research has been developing. Many writers on culture complain that researchers have worried too much about testing highly structured conceptual models with tightly quantitative procedures. They argue that this attempt provides only a crude, static snapshot of reality that does not explain the phenomena very well. Ott (1989) takes on this criticism and ties the new interest in culture to the growing interest in more qualitative research methods. These often involve going into organizations without preconceived ideas and carefully observing events and behaviors. Culture theorists argue that this approach more accurately analyzes organizational reality and prevents the misconceptions and inaccuracies that may arise out of the use of standard surveys and heretofore-conventional techniques. One cannot genuinely understand organizations and their successes and failures, they contend, without effective analysis of their cultures (Rainey, 1991).

One approach to understanding cultures within organizations is Schein's (1985) model of levels of cultures and their interactions within the organization. Important cultural elements, such as the physical layout of an organization's offices, the rules of interaction that are taught to newcomers, the basic values that come to be seen as the organization's ideology or philosophy, and the underlying conceptual categories and assumptions that enable people to communicate and interpret everyday occurrences contain many subtle clues that can lead to understanding the culture. Schein's model of cultures and their interactions can usefully be applied to SSA's cultural characteristics, such as its public service orientation and its bureaucratic complexity.

Schein's model has three different elements: artifacts, values, and basic assumptions. The first level, artifacts, is the most visible level of the culture as it includes its constructed physical and social environment. At this level, one can look at physical space, the technological output of the group, its written and spoken languages, artistic productions, and the overt behavior of its members.

The second level, values, represents the sense of "what ought to be," as distinct from "what is." When a group faces a new task, issue, or problem, the first solution proposed to deal with it can only have the status of a value because there is not yet a shared basis for determining what is factual and real. Many values remain conscious and are explicitly articulated because they serve the normative moral function of guiding members of the group in how to deal with certain key situations.

The third level contains the basic assumptions of the organization. These evolve as solutions to problems that are repeated over and over again and taken for granted. The repetition of the work creates an accepted solution. It can hinder change because in order to learn something new, it requires resurrection, reexamination, and/or frame breaking. These assumptions are taken for granted and indoctrinated into new members of the organization. They can become invisible and part of the organizational psyche, "the way it is," rather than "the way it should be."

Artifacts

The most visible aspect of Schein's model consists of its artifacts. These include the physical space, language, and technological outputs of the organization. The central offices of the SSA's Southern Region occupy a large office-building complex, but the interior design is modest and the offices are cramped. The security detail is highly visible. The language used within the agency is filled with acronyms. The first day I arrived at the agency, I completely misunderstood many of the conversations because I was not familiar with the jargon. As with most new members of the agency, I had to be provided with a document translating these words into terms I could understand by placing them in their proper context. Appendix B shows an example of this translation process.

SSA has many specific characteristics that are commonly accepted within the organization. They are continuously measuring the outputs of their work, from processing times to the amount completed. The measurements are continually reviewed and used to justify expenses or to request additional appropriations. The regional staff operations revolve around ensuring that the national objectives are met and dealing with problems. Most often the problems are ethical issues, personnel performance, or internal political turf battles.

Values

As described in Schein's model the second level of an organization's culture is its values. The value of public service orientation is immediately obvious within SSA. Public administration practitioners and educators have long contended that public employees are different from employees in other sectors of

American society (Perry and Porter, 1982). In fact, an increasing number of empirical studies suggest that public employees differ from their private sector counterparts with respect to work-related values and needs. For example, Wittmer (1991) analyzed differences in the rankings of eight reward categories for a sample of 210 employees in public, private, and hybrid organizations. He found the public and private employees differed significantly with respect to preferences for higher pay, helping others, and status. He concluded, "the public service ethic appears to be alive and well…[and] extends beyond core public organizations (government) to more hybrid groups" (1991, 380). Wittmer's findings reinforce the results of earlier empirical research by Rawls, Ulrich, and Nelson (1979), Rainey (1982), and Nalbandian and Edwards (1983). The pattern of findings is consistent with Perry and Porter's (1982) conclusion that the public motivation context is indeed different from that found in the private sector.

Conventional wisdom and empirical evidence indicating that public employees operate under different assumptions than those working in the private sector led Perry and Wise (1990) to define a construct for public service motivation (PMS) intended to capture the difference. They defined PMS as an individual's predisposition to respond to motives grounded primarily or uniquely in public institutions. Four dimensions – attraction to public policy making, commitment to the public interest and civic duty, compassion, and self-sacrifice – are empirically associated with the construct (Perry, 1996). A pamphlet written by an SSA employee from South Florida illustrates how he has directly helped beneficiaries. He writes, "The key word in SSA is service; service to the public is our job, and we feel proud. The main concern of the agency is to administer the program efficiently, and to provide courteous, sensitive and dignified service to the public" (Paulos, 1996).

My first experience with SSA as an organization was at a management conference in 1994 in Atlanta. The conference was attended by a majority of the management staff of the Southern Region. It was a two-day event organized by the regional office staff aimed at "energizing the troops," transmitting information, and getting feedback from the field. What really intrigued me was not that here was a room full of bureaucrats goofing off at government expense, but rather a group of people that believed their function was to help people and that their responsibility was not to be taken lightly. As the conference open, the theme was on "World Class Service." "We need to focus on our customers, the American Public", were the opening remarks of the regional commissioner, Gordon Sherman "Social Security is more than a program, it is a way of life. Only by extending our hands can we help the economic security of our nation" (Sherman, 1994).

As I interned in the regional office, the focus on public service was apparent. What makes this an apparent cultural characteristic is the impact that the programs of the agency have on the public. The programs administered by SSA ensure economic security for a great many Americans. When new recruits are brought into the agency, they undergo an intensive training program. This program addresses both broad and specific issues faced by SSA. One important objective is to indoctrinate these new employees with a belief in the importance of SSA. The program has become a fundamental part of the American way of life.

I participated in several orientation sessions as the organizers focused on explaining the broad general operational objectives and then moved on to teach the more detailed technical skills the new recruits would need. The administration of the individual programs can be defined as "cook book" public administration. When someone needs a benefit, you match the circumstances to the specific predefined options and then adjudicate the decision. This can become very tedious and mundane and there is pressure to process more claims to improve the individual statistics. In the retirement program alone, the influence on society can be seen. For individuals over sixty-five, currently one out of every ten is below the poverty level. Without SSA, that ratio would be one in two. A significant number of individuals are dependent on this program.

Within SSA, many of the employees refer to themselves as part of the SSA "family," which is even more apparent when observing the relationships between them. These strong relationships are particularly apparent in the field offices, where individuals tend to take on a personal responsibility for the programs they administer. They regularly go beyond the requirements of their jobs and are actively involved in the community. Outside their regular responsibilities, the managers and personnel of the field staff are actively involved in making their community a better place and improving the quality of life within the community. For instance, in an internal report on the Ocala, Florida office, there were statements about the staff's and management's participation in the United Way, Girl Scouts, Community Health Service, and Habitat for Humanity, all of which served to create "a positive image of SSA in the public eye while enriching those who participate" (Ocala, Florida Manager's Presentation Report, 1998). During the Christmas season, they assist the Santa on Wheels program and have sent boxes of clothes to Bosnia.

The regional newsletter also highlights employees who are involved in the community and constantly work to give a face to SSA. SSA is more than a program; it is a way to help others help themselves. When interviewing these civil servants, the core commitment to the program is very evident. To many, it is more than a job; it is a means to contribute to society in a positive way (Ban, 1995). As Richard Lytle, a Field Office Manager writes in his presentation report, "Richard enjoys the challenges of today's environment in SSA with all the opportunities for growing and learning. He and the management staff are looking forward to continue implementing changes through team work and cooperation at work and in his community (Ocala, Florida Manager's Presentation Report, 1998, p. 3). This level of commitment to the programs and to the agency may explain the longevity of the tenure of employees at SSA. They average over twenty years of government service and began their careers in the field (SSA, 1997). Most of the individuals who work in SSA have a social work background and seek to actively assist individuals in the community.

The Southern Region has also had a good track record when compared with other regions. Out of 50 million beneficiaries nationally, the Southern Region processes a bit over 10 million and nationally over 31 billion dollars are paid in monthly payments, of which 6 billion are accounted by the Southern Region (Harmon, 1997). The region has the highest workload and the best performance (Dyer, 1996) which gives members of the Southern Region a sense of pride. One other reason why the focus on public service is stronger in the Southern Region is its location. The Southern Region encompasses the eight southern states and within the south there is a very apparent trait known as "southern hospitality." "This trait is something that has made the role of treating the customer in a better way easier than that found in offices located in the northern part of the country, for example. Northerners tend to be more direct and to the point with people, which may appear to outsiders to be a lack of courtesy" commented Dr. Chater (1997). In my discussions with SSA Commissioner, Dr. Chater, characterized this as one of the most distinct reasons why different regions perform differently. She further commented:

> The culture of the local area puts an emphasis on different means to solve the problems of the local community. For instance, an example would be how to relate to diverse ethnic groups. The north has a faster paced lifestyle and everyone is in a hurry, while in the south there seems to be more civility coupled with a laid back attitude. This can also be seen in the interactions between different ethnic groups be they Hispanic, African American, or Native Americans (Chater, 1997).

Educating the public about SSA is vital to the longevity of the program and there is a very strong commitment to outreach within the community. SSA's public affairs officers regularly speak to groups in their communities promoting the virtues of the agency. Over three million young people under the age of 19 receive SSA checks each month. Of these, almost two million receive survivors' benefits because one parent has died; and more than one million receive disability benefits because a parent has become too disabled to work. Most Americans are associated with the program by either making a contribution to the program from every paycheck or by knowing or being a beneficiary. Educating the public helps explain why this social insurance is important.

One way to reach the community is an SSA developed teacher's kit, "Social Security and You." This program has become a popular learning tool in high school classrooms. Teachers are making use of the kit to help students understand the social insurance system that will affect them for the rest of their lives. The kit has been designed to be comprehensive and give teachers flexibility in fitting the lessons into their curriculum to meet the needs of the students. As one public affairs officer commented, "The teacher's kit gets students to start thinking about how they should be including Social Security in their financial planning

long before retirement. It helps them prepare for the future" (Patterson, 1998)

In South Florida, courses focusing on SSA have been developed and are taught by SSA employees.

They are targeted toward the high school and college-age audience. In one particular high school, they have

an end-of-the-year banquet that recognizes the students who excel in this SSA course. "This is a way to

ensure that the next generation of leaders is able to continue the much needed support of this American

institution," commented Patty Patterson, the deputy public affairs officer. All of these activities are

attempts to continually focus on the needs of the customer and to show the agency in the best possible

light. In the Southern Region, there is a strong commitment to the personnel and staff. There are

development programs, awards recognitions, and rituals that help support a nurturing environment. The

employees found within SSA have a strong commitment to the programs. These close relationships lead to

a high number of individuals who are personally committed to public service and the service of others.

Basic Assumptions

When a solution to a problem works repeatedly, it comes to be taken for granted. The work within

SSA is repetitive and tedious, with a certain standardization to the process. When visiting the field offices,

there is a strong emphasis on the uniformity of the decisions made regarding the claims processed. The

SSA employees pride themselves on their public service and continuous work to assist individuals who

come to seek assistance from the agency. With the pressure to continually increase their workloads,

individual workers are focused on moving each claim through the application process and then moving on

to the next. However, this can hinder a focus on individual circumstances and this is where a conflict most

frequently arises.

SSA's cultural value of being a public service oriented organization is a good match for the NPR

policy, particularly as NPR puts a significant emphasis on customer service. The executive order signed by

President Clinton directing them to provide customer service standards forced the agency to re-examine the

importance of the customer (Executive Order 12862, 1993). SSA has always been concerned with the customer, but what NPR made the agency do was to re-examine its approach. Customer expectations are changing, and could be better met by the agency. This was done by conducting customer service surveys, which reflected what the beneficiaries wanted.

In an interview, Larry Dewitt (1997), the SSA historian, stated that this "was a significant shift that occurred within the agency. SSA has always been a collector of data, but to focus on the needs of the customers was a new approach to meeting the expectations of the public. The public wanted expanded services on the 800 number, they wanted to be able to have more convenience when dealing with the agency, and they wanted more options when dealing with the agency, rather than simply face to face encounters".

When reviewing the changes that were needed within the agency, they were facilitated by the agency's public service orientation that the best way to serve the public is the only way. This value that is found within the SSA does facilitate the success of NPR. NPR's focus is on making sure that government agencies' actions result in meeting the needs of the customer. Because SSA is a service-oriented organization, this is a much simpler task than, for example, for the Department of Labor or the Department of Education. Their objectives and organizational purpose are not directly tied to dealing with the public. Another advantage that SSA possesses over other federal agencies is that the impact of its programs can be statistically measured

One example of the way NPR has shifted the focus more towards the customer are the improvements in SSA's 800 number telephone service. One of the tele-service centers is located within the Southern Region, in Birmingham, Alabama. This tele-service center is responsible for handling the calls made to the 800 number. This service was created before the inception of NPR, but was in an area that had room for improvement. After intensive customer service surveys, the results indicated that individuals were not concerned whether their phone call was answered on the first ring, as SSA encouraged, but were more interested in having their questions answered in a proper and timely manner. This led to a better training program being implemented and a change of focus from answering on the first ring to trying to answer or solve the problem within the first five minutes. This simple change in focus had a big effect on SSA's ability to better meet the demands of the public.

Bureaucracy

Government is an increasing part of the daily life of the average citizen. When studying public institutions, several characteristics describe them, one such being *bureaucratic* (Wilson, 1989). Commonly, being bureaucratic takes on a negative tone of red tape, layers of hierarchy, and inefficiency. Within public administration, bureaucracy is an attempt to create accountability and control in administering policy. The role of public bureaucracy does have an impact on the citizens they serve. Under Schein's (1985) model, its bureaucratic nature can be deemed a basic assumption of the way that SSA conducts its business.

In my association with SSA, I can best describe SSA as having two different types of individuals who make up the organization. There are the political appointees, who want to bring about a change and have a political agenda. The other group consists of career civil servants who can be subdivided into two groups, management and support staff. The Executive level includes all the deputy commissioners, regional commissioners, and top brass. One high ranking official described this group as "feudal kings." They all have their own little kingdoms and they are dominant in these areas. They are willing to discuss general directions, but pretty much operate using their own style. Their attitude can be summed up as "Don't mess with me and I won't mess with you" (Torrado, 1997). These individuals have seen initiatives come and go and are willing to adjust accordingly. As one staff member told me, the rule of thumb is that the organization does what the boss checks (Shiply, 1997). The other level is the field and support staff, who are committed public servants, but do not get too involved in the upper level politics of the organization. This group does their job and simply tries to keep up with the heavy workload that they are expected to take care of each day. When I was visiting a field office in Montgomery, Alabama, an unidentified claims representative shared her thoughts of NPR and the strategic plan. Her opinion of the daily work life was to "keep the files off my desk." At this street level bureaucrat (Lipsky, 1980), there is a strong disregard for NPR or the agency business plan. The bureaucrat is focus on what is going on in their office and not agency wide. When reviewing the history of SSA, the agency has evolved over its existence through several eras of tremendous growth and progress. These changes have arisen largely as a result of the introduction of new programs. The agency began as a simple retirement program, then came disability, and lastly Medicare. All these are major responsibilities and each added layers to the already existing hierarchy.

Three sources of decision making exist within the agency: the Commissioner's office, the central office bureaucracy, and the regional offices. They are all interconnected, but at the same time independent from each other. The authority also flows down through many layers of staff. With this high degree of hierarchy, an environment is created that allows for a constant "blame game" to be conducted when something does not get done.

SSA is an agency that measures everything, but it does not do a good job of fully utilizing this data. It measures processing time, workloads, and everything imaginable. An important obstacle to progress is the attempt to process this enormous amount of data in order to produce any meaningful results, creating an environment with a lot of motion, but little action. The agency is also very traditional in the way in which it administers the program. One high level officer expressed this by saying "SSA's success has also been its failure." The agency has continually produced results but has failed to focus on a corresponding constant improvement in quality. This can be at least partly attributed to being convinced of its continued success (Gracie, 1997).

"The wave of retirements has led to diminishing human capital and institutional expertise throughout the federal government," argues David Walker, the current Comptroller General and director of the General Accounting Office, "As today's leaders of government, we need to seek new qualified recruits to improve the federal workforce" (Walker, 1998). SSA faces the largest workload in its history with too few employees. During the coming years, SSA's retirement processing workload is projected to increase by one-fifth as the oldest of the 77 million baby boomers enter their 60s. At the same time, the disability workload is projected to rise by one-half as the rest of the baby boomers hit ages at which they are more likely to file disability claims. By 2020, the retirement workload will increase by one-half and the disability workload by three-fourths over current levels. Meanwhile, claims under SSI are expected to grow by one-fifth (Yoder, 2001). With the average age of agency employees on the rise, it also prevents new ideas and initiatives from being introduced and embraced by the staff. SSA is a good example of an aging organization that now has a lot of inbreeding in the hierarchies. The average age of staff at the managerial level is 49 and the overall age of agency employees is 47, (with over 20 years of service). Most of the current leaders of the agency have been promoted from within the organization. By 2010, 28,000 of its current 65,000 workers will be eligible to retire. Taking into account the 10,000 staff that are expected to leave in the next nine years for other reasons, the agency will have to replace more than half its workforce just as it is trying to cope with increased workloads and new technologies (Yoder, 2001). This combination of factors makes it hard for SSA to be receptive to dramatic organizational change.

After working within SSA, my view of government can be summarized in two broad observations: first, government workers are dedicated and believe they are providing for the common good; second, most production of goods and services by government is hopelessly constrained by customs, rules, and managers who are avoiding problems rather than solving them. SSA is a highly bureaucratic organization and fits well with NPR's goal of "cutting red tape." The 1994 federal workforce-restructuring act required the executive branch to cap employment at 1,922,300 for 1998, with a 15:1 ratio of employees to supervisors. Overall, in comparison to budget projections the Clinton administration eliminated 67,000 more positions than were required by the act (Gore, 1996; GAO, 1996d). Within SSA, this has been achieved by preventing new hires and eliminating jobs that become vacant. Within the Southern Region, many departments and responsibilities have been consolidated. One clear example is that the state directors now report directly to the regional commissioner, rather than the assistant regional commissioner for management and operations. This removes an entire layer of bureaucracy and gives directors a direct link to a major decision-maker.

This chapter covered the first three propositions that focused on implementation, leadership styles, and organizational culture. The next chapter will cover the last two propositions that focus on organizational culture followed by the conclusion.

Chapter 7 Consequences of National Partnership for Reinventing Government (NPR) for the Southern Region of the Social Security Administration (SSA)

"No executive branch reform in the twentieth century – indeed, perhaps in the Constitution's 210 years – has enjoyed such high level attention over such a broad range of activities for such a long period of time.".
Don Kettl, Brookings scholar

The Social Security Administration (SSA) is primarily responsible for ensuring the timely and accurate payment of billions of dollars in benefits. This high profile agency has always been subject to varying degrees of external pressure. Historically, the agency's constant challenge has been to react to legislative and judicial changes in SSA policy while simultaneously dealing with a continually revolving political and administrative leadership. Such changes seldom require major organizational overhauls within the agency, but they have produced a series of incremental shifts in procedure. The National Partnership for Reinventing Government (NPR) is one such external force designed to promote change within the federal government.

In this chapter, the final two propositions of this study are explored. The first is that NPR did create organizational change within the Southern Region of SSA. The second is that SSA continually faces changes created by the shifting demands on the agency. A brief review of the policy outcome of NPR also is explored. Finally, this chapter concludes by focusing on the contribution made by this dissertation to the study of public administration issues and suggest future avenues of study.

Proposition 4 -That NPR did create organizational change within the Southern Region of SSA

This research question is probably the most important because it evaluates whether there was a real change in the Southern Region of SSA due to the NPR initiative. NPR is specifically geared toward reforming federal government agencies. In general, NPR mandates that government agencies scrutinize their operations and seek more cost effective ways of doing business and enhancing public service. The NPR policy was initiated by the President and imposed throughout the entire executive branch. The key question is: did it meet the defined expectations and create change?

Organizational Change

Within the SSA organizational structure, regional offices are responsible for supporting the administration of SSA programs. These broad duties encompass daily administrative operations, human resources, and policy direction. The regional office staff does not have direct contact with the public, but they indirectly influence the interface with the public through the policies they set.

The head of the region is the Regional Commissioner (RC). This position has an executive staff that includes the deputy RC, the executive officer, state directors and executive assistants. The rest of the personnel at the regional office level are divided and subdivided into units that are responsible for specific duties, as shown in Figure 1 found in Chapter Three. Reviewing the organization structure before and after NPR, clear changes can be discerned between figure 7.1 and 7.2.

Figure 7 1 Southern Regional Organizational Chart Pre-National Partnership for Reinvention (NPR)

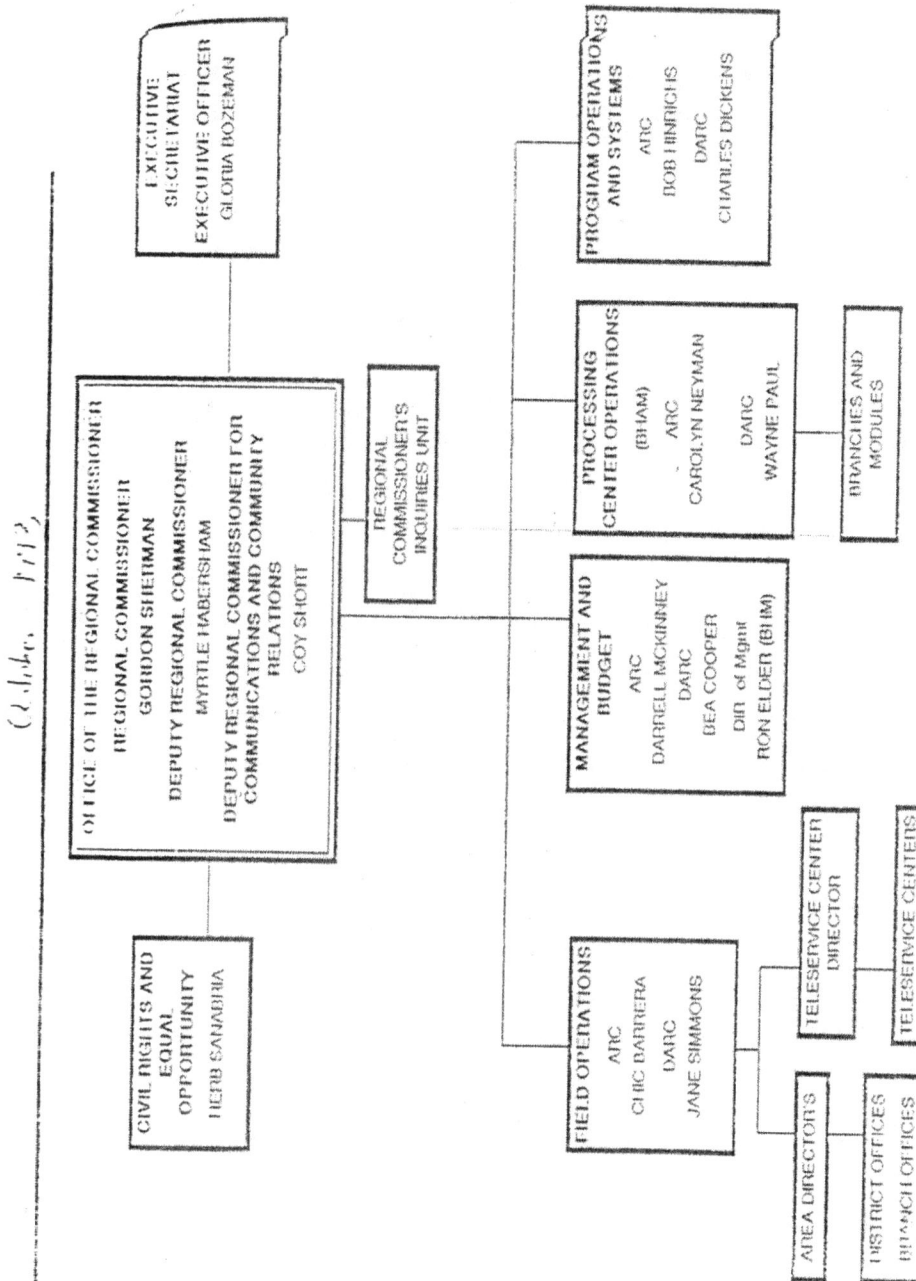

Figure 7 2 Southern Regional Organizational Chart Post-National Partnership for Reinvention (NPR) Changes

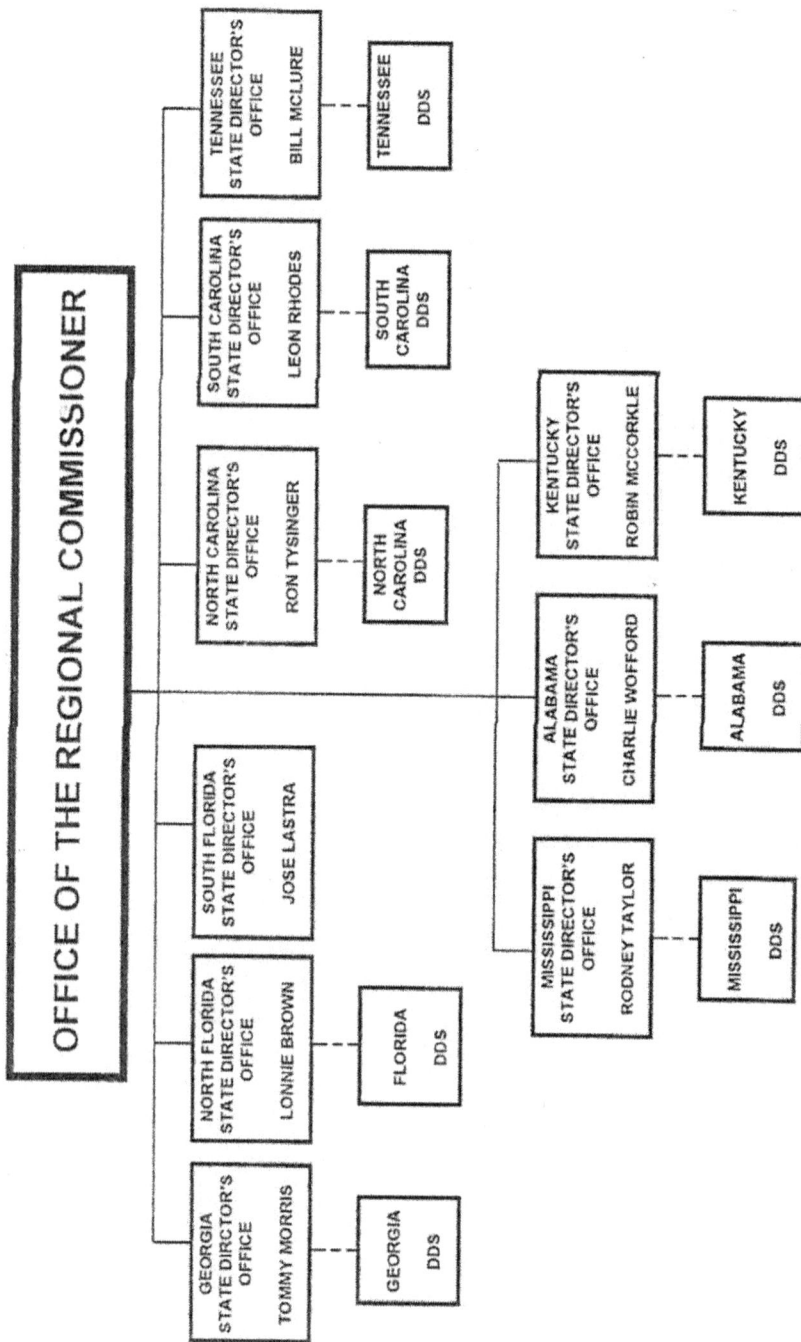

The chain of command has been modified to condense positions and concentrate responsibilities within management. This change resulted from the executive order mandating targeted management to staff ratios. A radical proposal that was discussed but not implemented was to consolidate regions, which would have immediately eliminated all the regional office staff and lowered management to staff ratios nationally. The political climate prevented this move from being a viable option (Spencer, 1997). However, downsizing and reclassifying positions made the agency more effective (Wood, 1997). A major impact of NPR was the mandate to reduce staff positions and increase the number of positions directly involved in case processing, in order to streamline the decision making process in the field (Ponder, 1997).

The Southern region is unique among the SSA's ten regions. It covers the largest region, is the most diverse, and has the largest workloads. For example, South Florida alone has more beneficiaries than both the Seattle and Kansas regions combined. This highlights the importance of the Southern region and its level of responsibility.

Within the Southern Region, some overt changes were apparent. One example that forced a significant shift in the operations of the regional office was the broadening of responsibilities specified by job classification. This enabled individual employees to be more flexible in performing their duties. Streamlining the agency led to less management oversight and required more attention to communications within the organization (Warden, 1996).

With the focus on streamlining government, one example of how the Southern Region moved to consolidate duties was the introduction of a "team" model to the units. This team model shifted the rigid lines within the chain of command, redefining the role of supervisor to that of team leader. An indirect result of this shift was that the boxes within the organizational chart were moved but the duties of each individual were not. Defining roles, responsibilities, and levels of authority was not only the most universally agreed upon need, but also the most problematic to address.

The question of "re-engineering" organizational standing is also important in the context of communications. In that regard, virtually all vested parties are of the opinion that re-engineering should fall under normal operational line responsibility (Dyer, 1996). Since this is a national SSA initiative, however, the region is obliged to follow the existing agency position as far as reporting lines are concerned. Although there are mixed opinions (Dyer, 1996) as to whether NPR initiatives have had an adverse impact upon normal case processing operations, there must be some mechanism in place for ongoing assessment.

The regional office focused on bringing the numbers down to the level required by NPR, ensuring that the 15:1 target ratio was achieved. This was not universally popular within the agency, as within the culture of SSA a position on the regional office staff carries a higher level of prestige and is seen as a more desirable place to work than the field offices. As one staff member commented, "In the field offices you had to deal with the public and have a mountain of paper work to deal with. Yes we have lots of responsibilities, but you do not deal with the hounding demands of the public who has high expectations" (Barrera, 1997).

One example of a new initiative designed with the aid of the NPR guidelines was the introduction of the Atlanta Region pilot program of the "State Directors Concept" on October 1, 1994. Georgia and North Carolina were the initial pilot states. The objective of the pilot was to improve the effectiveness of the agency's disability programs by placing internal responsibility for both state and federal aspects of the disability program in one location for each state. Streamlining the decision-making and oversight aspects of the program was expected to simplify the process. Breaking down barriers to innovations aimed at improving the disability program and allowing the SSA employees and the state DDS employees to work as full partners would encourage the development of a closer working relationship between the DDS administrators and the state directors (Warden, 1996).

In a memo to the regional commissioner, the Mississippi State Director wrote,

"SSA's reengineering initiative in conjunction with the NPR is analyzing every agency component with a view toward streamlining, delayering, cost effectiveness, etc. There is no component nor work activity excluded from scrutiny. We must grasp this concept as we begin effecting changes that will allow us to deliver World Class Service in a new and ever changing environment. I believe this is the impetus for the implementation of the State Director concept."(Taylor, 1997).

Another area of change seen in the organizational charts was a significant change in the way the region operated. This is most apparent for the state directors. Instead of reporting to the Assistant Regional Commissioner for Management and Operations Systems (ARC-MOS), they now report directly to the Regional Commissioner (RC). Removing a layer of administrative oversight had two immediate results: while the state directors became more accountable for their areas, the Regional Commissioner now had to deal with more localized administrative concerns. As one state director explained, "This allowed us to bring issues directly to the RC without being filtered through the ARC-MOS." As a result, the state directors had more authority to initiate much needed change within their states (Barrera, 1997).

In May 1995, the Disability Determination System (DDS) budget support function was internally transferred from the center for disability operations to the center for fiscal and property management. As a result of the Commissioner's decision on December 22, 1995, regional reorganizations were executed. New standard position descriptions (SPDs) were established for most positions, for GS-12s and above. On October 1, 1996, the State Directors concept was expanded to three additional states- South Carolina, Tennessee, and Alabama.

Effective March 1, 1997, the remaining three states, Florida. Mississippi, and Kentucky, were phased into the State Director concept. Since there are actually two state directors (SDs) in Florida, the North Florida SD assumed the primary liaison role with the State DDS Administrator; the South Florida SD works closely with the North Florida SD and serves in a parallel capacity with respect to the Miami satellite DDS sites (Barrera, 1997). There are several unusual operational features of the Florida disability workload. The area comprises approximately 28% of the regional workload and it has a decentralized profile, with 6 processing offices spread throughout the state. Additional SSA support has been provided by an SSA employee stationed in Tampa.

In mid-February 1997, the region conducted an orientation session for the directors of the final three states to make the transition. During this session, Regional Commissioner Sherman provided additional guidance and direction. For example, he indicated that changes should be more consistent with a sharing of responsibility than a transfer of responsibility. He further stated that it would be critical to develop good working relationships among all parties; regional office program employees are very capable, and staff to staff contact on cases should be a workable proposition. DDS administrators should have the latitude to call whomever handles a particular functional area (Sherman, 1997). He reminded the group that any changes proposed or taken must be considered within the scope of SSA's general effort to increase staff to management ratios and to streamline the decision making process. He was also reiterated that there must be no increase in overall staff levels at the offices of each state director as a result of these changes (Sherman, 1997).

The SDs at the orientation session agreed that "reengineering should fall under the line management control of operations." Good communication between the components would be essential to the ultimate success of the project. The issues of regional office components providing support to the offices of the state director was not a new and novel idea; this had been the case with all other regional office components for quite some time. Some of those interviewed felt that the current trend would be temporary in nature and, at some point, the initiative would fail and things would simply revert to the way they were before. However, there had been no internal indication whatsoever that SSA would some how be exempt from such mandates as streamlining, delivering, or decentralization of decision making. Nor had there been any suggestion that the agency was wavering in its support of the NPR initiative (Harmon, 1997b).

Other departments were also impacted by reorganization. One example is the Center for Human Resources (CHR), which had already made the shift from being a part of the Health and Human Services Department towards the independent agency status of SSA. They were responsible for the varying functions of human resources within the agency, including advertising positions, hiring new recruits, and employees' pay and benefits.

In an attempt to deal with the element of uncertainty inherent in the operation of the SSA, the concept of work teams was proposed. Created by an interdepartmental group, the work team concept provides the most appropriate model to get the work done. Human resource services are provided exclusively by established teams under the Center for Human Resources, providing "one stop shopping" to customers. The use of work teams makes it possible to reduce the number of structural and supervisory layers, empowering staff to deliver quality and timely service. The timetable established required immediate action and resulted in a team type environment consisting of four "one stop, full service" teams (The Atlanta Region Center for Human Resources, 1997).

Each team has only one team leader who is not considered to be part of the management tier, but facilitates the best use of the talents of the members of the team. The teams handle internal placement, special emphasis programs, employee benefits counseling, maintenance of files and records, employee Personnel processing (including awards and payroll errors caused by Personnel processing), employee and office classification, Department of Interior Employee Help Desk functions, and external recruitment. Geographical assignments determine team service areas. Each team's area assignment includes an office for hearings and appeals Field Offices. A regional office component is assigned to each team. Mail and receptionist functions are assigned to the office of the Director (The Atlanta Region Center for Human Resources, 1997).

Working in teams produces benefits for both team members and the organization in which they work. Overall, the organization has embraced the team concept, but in many ways it is still using specialized and outmoded techniques. Empowering employees is an effective means of encouraging individuals to be creative in their work. Yet, the tools for effective empowerment must be available and organizational support, continual training and education, and technological improvements are only a few of the tools needed by the employees.

The Center for Human Resources (CHR) is going through a period of transformation. In the last five years the Center has undergone several changes as a component agency within SSA and the difficulties inherent in this transformation have been compounded by the many concurrent advances in computer-based technology. Impact Program Service Centers and alternates on each team were expected to maintain the existing system until Department of Interior conversions were implemented (Spearman, 1996).

The reduction in the number of positions resulted in changes in classification for existing positions and elimination of staff levels. It is clear from executive staff notes that NPR was constantly a concern when reviewing weekly FTE (Full Time Equivalents) goals. When resources were available for new recruits, certain diversity quotas were set to be able to maintain a balance within the work force. However, the executive order mandating a reduction in the workforce adversely impacted the ability of the agency to hire new recruits. As a result, constant attempts were made to use creative means in order to attract new personnel. For instance, one method of bringing in new personnel was the scholars program. This program simplified the route by which new hirees could become a part of the agency. The qualifications were that the students have an overall grade point average of 3.5. The strong regulations issued by the Office of Personnel Management (OPM) created a scale to assess the merit of potential recruits. Highest priorities are assigned to those who are veterans, disabled, or have previous government service. Finally, developing specific job classifications could facilitate matching a particular job description to a candidate. Staff meetings discussions reviewed FTE allocations (Harmon, 1997d).

In the field, the changes were more apparent because achieving the 15:1 ratio was a major goal. Changes in the structure of the office staff were implemented and the titles and job descriptions that listed their responsibilities were reclassified. The proportion of management staff could not simply be reduced by attrition, although this would be the simplest and least painful way for the organization. However, considering the aging work force within SSA, the pace of retirements has risen significantly.

NPR's constant focus on reducing the size of government at all costs also had some negative impacts. One of the most significant was the way it reduced the SSA's flexibility and its ability to bring new blood into an already aging agency. Managers within the field were constantly concerned with the reduction in staff. In a memo, they pointed to several concerns:

Lack of support for field offices (FO) and FO management- Although we talk about redesigning processes, delegating to lower levels, streamlining management, etc., our actions do not support our words. We've gone through a paper process of having team leaders, yet nothing substantive occurred. As usual, FO's have suffered the impact [of] the downsizing while management outside FO's continue to exhibit a total lack of concern and understanding of the problems existent in the field. Managers in the field are truly on their own in a daily battle with the public, [with] ever increasing workloads, and an uncaring and irresponsible upper management team. (American Federation of Government Employees AFL-CIO, 1996).

A member of the executive staff notes:

We recognize that resources are limited in this era of downsizing government. We also recognize that systems enhancements have in the past, and will in the future, make it easier for us to do our work with smaller staffs. However Operations mangers increasingly report that they are unable to meet all of their varied responsibilities with the resources available to them today. This is true despite the increasing use of unpaid help, such as volunteers and work experience placements, who perform significant amounts of clerical work in many offices. We feel that the agency has lost its balance. We have reached a stage of crisis management in which the crise du jour gets all of our attention while the next problem festers until its day comes. Backlogged prisoner alerts were not addressed until the Bonin case hit the papers. Attorney fee petition backlogs became a concern only when advocates made public criticisms. Our customer service pledge is written in broad terms which apply to all of [the] services we provide. We believe that it is imperative that we act to improve our ability to handle all of our work (Harmon, 1998).

Within the Southern region there was organizational change within the formal organizational structure, although many of the informal structures still stood. Most of these changes were not able to reduce SSA's workloads. SSA is an agency that must react to the shifting demands of its environment, which is full of never ending obstacles.

Proposition 5- Social Security continually faces challenges caused by the shifting demands on the agency

Social Security has encompassed both the most successful and the most controversial federally-mandated programs. The organization has had to react to the demands created by external and internal forces. Historically, SSA has dealt with these challenges effectively. NPR can be credited with facilitating an internal change in the Southern Region, but change is part of the nature of SSA.

As discussed in chapter three, SSA has always been a hotbed of constant change. The evolution of SSA has progressed through genesis, evolution, maturation, and modernization. Three forces that have served as catalysts for this change are the expansion of the program, demographic changes, and concerns about its long-term solvency. The key to SSA was its reciprocal obligation (Ball, 2000).

Throughout the evolution of SSA, there have been significant changes to its programs. Initially, the program was created to provide a system of social insurance that would be a partial income replacement program. As time passed, other entitlements were added that changed the nature of the program. These additions were survival benefits, disability coverage, and supplementary social insurance. These new programs were deemed necessary by the policy makers as an attempt to assist American workers. As illustrated by countless examples during the history of the agency, SSA has been able to meet the ever-increasing demands of its growing constituency. Legislative action has resolved many of the previous conflicts. These changes have become a part of the agency culture, enabling it to deal with change effectively.

The make up of the workforce has changed over the history of SSA, and this is also a significant challenge facing the agency. The entrance of large numbers of women into the workforce has shifted the demographics of those contributing to SSA and placed an equitable need to cater to the needs of this part of the work force. The whole structure of society has changed and so has its economic needs.

An external factor that also produces constant shifts in SSA policy is the politicization of the agency. The policy makers in Congress and the executive branch react to the effective mobilization of mature voters during the election cycle and this sector of the electorate supports SSA. SSA has been referred to as the "third rail of politics" and the recent public discourse has resulted in a great deal of political rhetoric but no political action.

Perhaps the biggest challenge Social Security has to deal with is actually its internal concerns. As discussed in the previous chapter under the heading on bureaucracy, SSA's faces increased workloads and a workforce aging much faster than the people it serves.

The agency is facing a strong wave of change administratively due to the aging its workforce. SSA has reduced staffing by 25% within the last 15 years, while at the same time, increasing the scope and quality of the services offered to customers. Decreases in personnel in the 1980s have led to a void in the agency's organizational structure, with a lack of experienced staff ready to move up into the higher levels of the agency. Most senior executives in service are ready to retire and this has created a leadership vacuum, revealing a need for rising stars. As with any organization, the higher the level within the agency, the more responsibility and tougher the decisions that go with the job (Lelane, 1997). SSA is going through many of the same challenges that most other large bureaucracies are facing: diminishing resources, downsizing, and a rising level of expectations. These shifting forces serve as catalysts for change and an appropriate backdrop for NPR.

In the first NPR report, *Creating a Government that Works Better & Cost Less*, two of the major objectives listed are: putting customers first, and empowering employees to get results. These are the two of NPR's initial objectives that are most closely linked to the continual changes facing SSA.

The most direct effect of NPR within the Southern Region was to set a high priority on improving customer service. Even though the agency has always been a service-oriented agency, defining the customer had not previously been specifically identified (Carter, 1997).

As President Clinton stated in the presentation of the NPR report, "The federal government must be customer driven" (Clinton, 1993). In response to the NPR mandate of increased customer service, SSA sent a questionnaire to over 30,000 individuals. "Close to 50% of the barriers [to service] identified in the questionnaires had to do with staffing and that is understandable", says Toni Lelane. "Employees know that in the past 10 years, SSA's staffing has gone down 20% and that during the same time, the workload has gone up 30%. Employees, especially those on the front lines, are working under great stress, and it is probably hard to believe that meaningful improvement can come without some measure of staffing relief" (Lelane, 1997). The field office managers are now being held more accountable, and as workloads increase this forces them to make certain that they can meet the expected results (Morris, 1997). This has created an environment of being in "crisis mode," where staff deal with what is on the front burner at that particular moment rather than taking the long view and initiating innovative ways to make government work better.

One example of a change that has improved customer service is SSA's 1-800 toll-free telephone service. In the first report of NPR, Commissioner Chater made a pledge to President Clinton, "We are establishing standards for telephone service that include promptness, courtesy, and accuracy. Within industry as models, we are making progress. But we still have much to do. We believe we can give the American people the telephone service they deserve. We promise to work hard to achieve this goal and report to you in September 1995" (Gore 1994, p. 46)

An independent study conducted by Dalbar, Inc. designed to evaluate the telephone customer service levels delivered by nine companies, including services both from the private and public sector, found SSA to have the highest ranking in providing telephone customer service (Dalbar Financial Services, 1995; Gore 1995). As spelled out by the key findings within the report: "Representatives at the SSA displayed a unique ability to anticipate the caller's every need and provide the caller with appropriate information without having the caller articulate the request. Performance of this caliber placed the SSA first in the accommodation ranking. SSA representatives' ability to anticipate the caller's needs also had an impact on the scores for knowledge. The representatives understanding of the caller's needs translated into a clear and confident response to the caller's inquiry" (Harvey and DiCesare 1995, p. 4). A leading magazine, *Business Week* wrote, "Who'd have guessed the Social Security folks give better customer service on the phone than Corporate America's role models? Dalbar rated how long it rings, how long you're on hold, and how knowledgeable staffers are. Social Security did best on ring time- four seconds. L.L. Bean took 12 seconds to answer" (Business Week, 1995).

A federal consortium benchmark study was commissioned with NPR as a result of Executive Order 12862 (1993), *Setting Customer Standards*, which mandates that "All executive departments and agencies that provide significant services directly to the public shall benchmark customer service performance against the best in the business." This study identified successes and weakness within the toll free number system. The Southern Region was directly influenced by this decision because it administers the tele-centers in Birmingham, Alabama and Fort Lauderdale, Florida.

The report identified seven key components that comprise best practices, including: leadership strategies for success, information management and analysis, planning, human resource management, process management, business results, and customer focus and stratification (NPR, 1995). As an internal memo states, four key policy directives were proposed as a direct result of this report. These targets are: answering in 15-20 seconds and/or rarely allowing a busy signal, operating more hours a day and more days a year, giving accurate information, and giving front line employees authority to solve problems (Chater, 1995).

Within the Southern Region, the effects of changes aimed at improving the toll free service were very apparent. As explained by the deputy regional commissioner, "The 800 number is the key to deal with the diminishing resources of the agency. Only by centralizing our responsibilities can we be expected to meet our targeted numbers. Despite SSA's excellent toll free telephone services, we still need to improve. SSA field offices are becoming more crowded each day, and waiting times appear to be rising. One third of callers now get a busy signal or hang up in exasperation after long waits. The quality of claims decisions appears to be declining as workloads rise, thereby putting greater pressure on an already overburdened appeals process" (Fine, 1997). As a reaction to the increasing expectations from SSA's clientele, more resources were deployed within the tele-center operations. "Our customers seek to be able to make one phone call and get all their questions answered and handled by one point of contact. Today our operators do more, as a result of NPR, than they did just a few years ago" (Wilson, 1996).

The second objective outlined by the initial NPR report that dealt with the continual change within SSA is, "empowering employees to get results." As Gore explained in a speech, "Our long-term goals is to change the very culture of the federal government. A government that puts people first, puts its employees first too. It empowers them, freeing them from mind-numbing rules and regulations. It delegates authority and responsibility. And it provides for them a clear sense of mission" (Gore, 1993).

Creating a culture of learning organizations (Senge, 1995) is what the NPR is all about (Fairbrother, 1997). However changing the culture is a lot harder than merely changing a few rules and regulations. As one veteran of many government reform initiatives observed, "Changing government is a bit like moving the town cemetery. It's much harder to deal with the feelings it arouses than with the relocation itself" (Gore, 1993, p. 66).

Pressure to show that the region is producing good results and that this is at least partly due to the success of NPR is evident by the credit given to NPR. The buzzwords emerging from NPR have been posted everywhere: "make government work better and cost less". The emphasis on customer service was constantly reiterated at every opportunity by the higher-level staff members in the regional office. However, some of the examples cited as indicators of change were not actually due to NPR, but rather to the way SSA had shifted to using updated technologies.

It is not easy to discern to what extent NPR should get credit for improvements, as other initiatives are simultaneously underway within the agency. For instance, there were already plans in place to upgrade the technology within the field offices. However, NPR did facilitate a quicker implementation schedule. The IWS/LAN system, which is the new technology selected to create a better network system, was a result of Dorcus Harding's leadership in the Reagan administration. The installation of the hardware actually occurred during the Clinton administration, allowing NPR to cite it as a reinvention success even though it was already in the works before the NPR initiative was born (Barrera, 1997). The Clinton Administration was very supportive of new technology and this disproportionately favored new ideas utilizing the latest gadgets (Spencer, 1997).

Within the field offices, NPR was mentioned by the local office managers but did not directly influence daily operations. "Everyday my main objective is to make sure the office runs smoothly. Yes, there can be a better way to do things, but who has the time, I got deadlines and pressures from the regional office to meet my stated workload objectives (Brown, 1998). With all the fanfare of NPR, this is the most critical obstacle to overcome. How can a policy that is at the center of all pertinent discussions within the central and regional office be translated into the culture of the field offices? One solution to this obstacle for future policy initiatives can be the use of a policy net.

Empowering employees involves innovation within the workforce. One project that has the potential to enable agency policy to be developed in a way that best meets the demands of the field office is a pilot project named the "policy net". The Southern Region has been involved in its development and implementation. It is a program that allows input from all levels of the decision-making process using the Lotus Notes software. For example, a person in Baltimore can come up with a good idea and as it passes up through the chain of command, individuals can make comments and add suggestions for improvement, thus adding to the quality of the innovation. "The policy net has the potential to create real time decision making and enact the best administrative policy for each of the regions" (Chlumsky, 1997). The policy process allows information to be shared from the lowest to the highest levels.

The culture within the Southern Region has pockets of innovation. This has been shown by the numerous Hammer Awards received. One reason why this flexibility for innovation exists can be credited to its size. Atlanta performance goal is a result of management awareness of the current state of the workload. This enables them to shift personnel or take whatever action is necessary to expedite personnel or take what ever action is necessary to expedite processing. Their desire to perform has been heightened by the fact that they have been successful. Their expectation level is high and problems are few (SSA, 1998e),

By being the largest region and having the best performing region, innovation can be more manageable (Fine, 1997). The Hammer Award is the recognition designated by NPR to spotlight successes within the federal government. In an executive staff meeting, Sherman ascribes this success to the region's "focus on people and [ability to] create a group environment that develops teams to innovate and do things right" (Harmon, 1998).

SSA is an agency of change and has constantly maintained an often precarious balance between the old way and the new way. The role of NPR is important in allowing innovations in government to flourish because it has the support of the administration. Even though this is a good quality to have in an organization, there are limits to the number of new methods that can be implemented simultaneously. For example, the Denver and Dallas regions emphasized the entire workload process, but this initiative had to be scrapped once it was determined that these regions were not reaching their targeted objectives (Colvin, 1997). The bottom line is that it is results that count.

Policy Outcomes- What has been learned as a result of the NPR policy?

SSA is fortunate that the agency has a single, well-defined, well-integrated mission. The strategic goals and objectives are inherently complementary, and their interrelationships can be readily understood by the staff as well as by the stakeholders. In addition, most of SSA's goals and objectives have evolved over a long period of time. In one form or another, they have guided SSA planning and management for the past 66 years.

Government reforms are designed to change the old bureaucratic functions of government. The attempt to change SSA with a simple policy like NPR has been met with some skepticism. The most common criticism is that it is simply impossible to do so. There are too many difficult clients, internal conflicts, and little public confidence. However managing a large organization is the art of the possible, the art of finding the possible within what might be viewed as impossible pressures (Kanter, 1989). The second myth harks back to the theories of Frederic Taylor. He viewed organizations as essentially machines. He did not focus on the human dimensions of management, the personal challenges that many managers face.

His approach would lead a manager to believe that if you pull the right levers in the right way, you'll get the right result.

In complex organizations there can be failures for any number of reasons: poor communication, impractical or unclear goals, lack of public or congressional support, lack of sufficient expertise or resources, too much or too little oversight, and too much work. Between these extremes- where nothing works or everything can be made to work- lies some basic truths about large modern organizations.

According to congressional auditors, the reinventing government movement launched in 1993 was largely successful. According to a GAO (1998) report, ten federal agencies have fully or partially implemented over 90 percent of key administration recommendations for reinventing government. The agencies reported that 33 recommendations were fully implemented and another 30 were partly implemented. Still, NPR initiatives cannot be separated from other government reform efforts, particularly the 1993 Government Performance and Results Act (GPRA) and the oversight efforts of Congress. As the GAO (1998, p.14) report concludes, "An attempt to isolate the specific contributions that any one entity made to successful management reforms- or to apportion 'credit' among entities- is generally not possible."

NPR was effective in serving as a catalyst for the discussion of change. The key to its effectiveness within sectors of the organization depended on the administrative leadership and its ability to overcome organizational cultural barriers. More obvious limitations were that NPR objectives were too broad and that NPR was a continuation of previous government reform movements. Within the administration of NPR initiatives, the organization became too political due to its close ties to the administration. NPR's top down approach prevented the actualization of successful implementation where it mattered: the street level bureaucrat. A common criticism was that many of the successes that were touted as NPR successes were already part of other projects, and when subjected to closer scrutiny were not as successful as they originally appeared.

A GAO (1999) report outlines the challenges facing this assessment exercise as follows. Were these reductions apparent? The GAO was unable to substantiate the billions in savings claimed by the Clinton administration for Vice President Al Gore's project to streamline and "reinvent" government, according to federal auditors. The White House Office of Management and Budget (OMB) had no documentation for many of the asserted savings, and some savings had been double-counted according to the GAO, the nonpartisan investigative arm of Congress. (GAO, 1999, p 3)

Vice President Al Gore's NPR has claimed $137 billion in savings from reinvention since 1993. However, many of NPR's savings are suspect according to the GAO. The Office of Management and Budget, which is responsible for NPR's accounting, erred more than once and tried to take full credit for savings that were actually due to many factors rather than NPR alone, the GAO said in a recent report (GAO, 1999, p.13). "In general, the savings estimates we reviewed could not be replicated, and there was no way to substantiate the savings claimed," GAO said in their review of NPR's claims. However, this statement is challenged by OMB spokesperson Linda Ricci: "The report focuses on some fairly detailed, even arcane details about accounting. What's more important is that today government works better, more efficient and more cost-effectively" (Saldarini, 1999, p 6).

"Instead of reinventing government, it looks like they were reinventing accounting rules," said Rep. Dan Burton (R-ID), chairman of the House Committee on Government Reform. Burton, who requested the study, added, "I'm glad the vice president had made reinventing government a priority. However he shouldn't try to pad the numbers or take credit for savings that haven't happened."("Reinventing what?", 1999).

Discussion and Evaluation- Casting the results in the framework of Public Administration

Four areas of the public administration literature were addressed in the propositions developed in this dissertation. They are implementation, leadership, organizational culture, and organizational change. They comprise the most significant areas faced by the research presented in the study.

Policy Implementation

Holt (1993) observed that the two major implementation theories top-down and bottom-up, limit the implementation system to a two layer model, disregarding the multileveled networks that exist in reality.

It is clear that NPR's implementation followed a top-down approach. However, the program was touted as a quasi bottom-up approach that would empower the lower tier of the federal government to enact change. NPR did initiate change and create a shift in the course of activity within the agency.

The first proposition states that NPR objectives match SSA's mission and can be expeditiously implemented found that they complemented each other well. NPR sought better customer service and SSA is a customer focus agency. An accurate assessment of NPR's success depends on the measurement used. If a broad review attempts to check off items on a laundry list of accomplishments, then it has been a success. However, a deeper probe reveals a very different picture of an agency that has been effective in achieving its purpose but at the cost of focusing tightly on the immediate issues with a type of tunnel vision that excludes the peripheral view. NPR was a combination of political hype and good public relations. It did seek out and reward good examples of innovative government, but it also simply repackaged what had worked and named it a success under the auspices of NPR.

Leadership Styles

The proposition that stated that the effective implementation of NPR in the Southern Region was effective because of the leadership style of a long serving, established Regional Commissioner focuses on leadership issues. Effective leadership served as an important component of effectively utilizing the window of opportunity presented by NPR. NPR was able to encourage innovations in government to flourish because it had the support of a presidential administration that sought change within the federal structure. Effective leadership was very important for the successful implementation of NPR. The political nature of SSA can often hinder access to innovation and change. Within public administration, political forces play a significant role in policy development. There is no way to succeed in the environment of the federal government if the channels are not exploited to steer effectively the change needed. No one, whether on the bureaucratic or political side, can work in a vacuum. NPR opened a window of opportunity that the regional commissioners were able to utilize to implement some innovative practices within the organization.

It was another means of dealing with the atmosphere of diminishing resources and continual pressure to make government "work better and cost less."

Organizational Culture

Understanding the culture of the organization is equivalent to understanding the personality of the organization. When investigating the inner working of SSA, there can be few traits of its culture that facilitated the implementation of NPR. The organization is full of bureaucratic and political obstacles. However, SSA employees do have a commitment to helping others within the realm of public service. It is this trait that resonated with NPR's targets for improving customer service. The limitations are due to the constraints imposed by customs, rules, and management.

Changing the organizational culture is a long term effort. Two key techniques found within the Southern region are of prime importance to a successful culture change. First, top management must be totally committed to the change in both words and actions. NPR enjoyed a united front from the top managers within SSA. Second, organizations must provide training that promotes and develops skills related to their desired values and beliefs. This was begun somewhat by the continual leadership training based on the NPR's Human Resource Development Council (1997) findings published in the *Getting Results through Learning*. Both with the current culture and NPR's push toward making government "work better and cost less", organizational change within the Southern region began.

Organizational Change

The next proposition, that NPR did fostered Organizational Change is difficult to assess given the obstacles to measure change accurately. The very bureaucratic nature of SSA prevents any dramatic changes in the old methods of conducting the business of the organization. With so many examples touted by NPR, how can this change be long lasting?

SSA has always been able to adapt to the shifting pressures on the agency. This arguably is the reason why SSA has been able to sustain its long record of success. The focus on long term solvency and meeting its financial obligation forces the agency to reevaluate its footing. The continual emphasis on long lasting solvency has created an environment that needs to change with the evolving demographic profile of its customer base.

Issues for future research

Although this study addresses organizational change within a public institution, further work needs to be done to assess to what degree new public policies can create a framework of successful change. The saga of organizational change within the Southern Region is not finished. This study serves as a base for further research in this area because currently there is very little literature available that addresses the propositions. Based on the findings of the study, the following recommendations are made for future studies.

Despite an impressive growth in the quantity and quality of implementation research in recent years, such studies are typically either bottom up or top down. Often neglected in these two approaches is the actor caught between conflicting pressures from above and below. Thus, there is a need to combine elements of both the top-down and bottom-up frameworks into a single model of intergovernmental policy implementation which, in turn, could help provide us with a richer and more accurate understanding of the policy implementation process.

The SSA needs to increase its investment in strengthening and modernizing the way that it operates. At present, it tends too much toward the bureaucratic model and needs to move toward becoming a learning organization. Within the complex structure of the organization, there exist pockets of innovation. How can these areas of innovation be tapped and transformed agency wide? This would be a valuable understanding within the field of organizational theory.

The changing make up of the organization resulted from both the aging of the workforce and the way SSA is moving from being a civil servant led institution to one that reacts to the rapidly changing political climate. More of the top leaders within the organization are political appointees than traditional civil servants. These influences determine the dynamics of the organization.

Conclusion

Four lessons have been learned from this study. NPR was implemented in a top down fashion. The culture of SSA did significantly influence the implementation of NPR. The effective implementation of NPR in the Southern Region was in part a result of the effective administrative leadership of the regional commissioner in nurturing innovative methods for administering SSA programs. Finally, government reform movements are a way to promote internal change within large bureaucratic government organizations.

SSA has always been able to weather the storm of external pressures from the constant changes of focus from Presidential administration to Presidential administration. Even though NPR did have an influence on the delivery of the programs within the Southern Region, opinions are mixed as to whether NPR did meet its expectations or simply served as part of the ever-changing environment within a complex public institution. As is true in most organizations, within SSA the more things change, the more they stay the same.

References

Achenbaum, W. Andrew. 1986. *Social Security: Visions and Revision.* New York: Cambridge University.

Advisory Council on Social Security. 1997. *Findings and Recommendations, 1994-1996 Advisory Council on Social Security.* Washington, DC: US Government Printing Office.

Altmeyer, Arthur J. 1966. *The Formative Years of Social Security.* Madison: The University of Wisconsin Press.

American Discuss Social Security (ADSS). 1998. *Making Sense of Social Security: A Discussion Starter.* Washington, DC: Pew Charitable Trust.

Anderson, James E. 2000. *Public Policy Making: An Introduction.* Boston, MA: Houghton Mifflin Company.

Argyris, Chris. 1996. *Organizational Learning II: Theory, Method, and Practice.* Reading, Mass.: Addison Wesley Pub. Co.

Armstong, Barbara N. 1932. *Insuring the Essentials, Minimum Wage Plus Social Insurance A living Wage Program.* New York: McMillian.

Arnold, Peri. 1995. Reforms changing Role. *Public Administration Review.* 55: 407-417.

Baldwin, J.N. 1987. Public Versus Private: Not that different, not that Consequential

Public Personnel Management. 16: 181-193.

Ball, Robert M. 2000. *Insuring the Essentials: Bob Ball on Social Security.* Washington, DC: The Century Foundation.

Ball, Robert M. 1998. *Straight Talk about Social Security: An Analysis of the issue in the current debate.* New York: Century Freedom Press.

Ban, Carolyn. 1995. *How do Public Mangers Manage? Bureaucratic Constraints, Organizational Culture, and the Potential for Reform.* San Francisco: Jossey-Bass.

Barnard, Chester I. 1938. *The Functions of An Executive.* Cambridge: Harvard University Press.

Barnes, Louis. 1967. Organizational Change and Field Experiment Methods. In *Methods of Organizational Research.* Victor Vroom, ed., pp. 57-111. Pittsburgh: University of Pittsburgh Press. Bass, B.M. 1985. *Leadership and Performance Beyond Expectations.* New York: Free Press.

Bennis, Warren G. 1959. Leadership Theory and Administrative Behavior: The Problem of Authority. *Administrative Science Quarterly.* 4:259-260.

Bennis, Warren G. 1989. *On Becoming a Leader.* Massachusetts: Addison-Wesley Publishing Company.

Bennis, Warren G. 1997. *Organizational Genius: secrets of creative collaboration.* Reading, Mass: Addison-Wesley Publishing Company.

Berkowitz, Edward D. 1995. *Mr. Social Security: The Life of Wilbur J. Cohen.* Kansas: University of Kansas.

Blau, Perter M. 1955. *The Dynamics of Bureaucracy.* Chicago: University of Chicago Press.

Bowsher, Charles A. 1992. Meeting the New American Management Challenge in a Federal Agency. *Public Administration Review.* 52: 3-7.

Bozeman, B and S. Loveless. 1987. "Sector Context and Performance: A Comparison of Industrial and Government Research Units". *Administration and Society.* 19: 197-235.

Broder, John M. "Clinton, with Crisis swirling puts focus on Social Security in upbeat State of the Union Talk". *New York Times*, 28 January 1998, A1.

Brudney, Jeffrey L., Laurence J. O'Toole, and Hal Rainey. 2000. *Advancing Public Management: New Developments in Theory,* Washington, DC: Georgetown University Press.

Burns, Eveline and Mable Richardson. 1956. *Social Security and Public Policy.* New York: McGraw Hill.

Burns, James MacGregor. 1978. *Leadership.* New York: Harper & Row.

Burns, Tom. 1966. *Industrial Man.* London: Penguin Publications.

Burns, Tom and G.M. Stalker. 1961. *The Management of Innovation.* London: Tavistock.

Burrell, Gibson and Gareth Morgan. 1979. *Sociology Paradigms and Organizational Analysis.* London: Heinemann.

Business Week. 1995. "To Scream, press '0'". *Business Week,* May 29.
Cameron K, Sutton, R.I. and Whetten, DA (eds). 1988. *Readings in Organizational Decline.* Mass: Ballinger.

Carlson, R.V. & Awkerman, G. 1991. *Educational Planning: Concepts, Strategies and Practice.* New York: Longman Press.

Carnevale, David G. 1995. *Trustworthy Government: Leadership and Management Strategies for Building Trust and High Performance.* San Francisco: Jossey-Bass.

Carter, Marshall N. and William G. Shipman. 1996. *Promises to keep: Saving the Social Security's Dream*. Washington, DC: Regnery Publishing.

Chadler, Alfred D., Jr. 1962. *Strategy and Structure*. Cambridge, Mass: The M.I.T. Press.

Chater, Shirley. 1994. Speech to Managers Regional Meeting. Atlanta, Georgia. August 10, 1994.

Cleveland, Harlan. 1985. *The Knowledge Executive: Leadership in and Information Society*. New York: Truman Talley Books.

Clinton, Bill. 1993. Remarks on presentation of first NPR report. White House: Washington, DC. September 7, 1993.

Clinton, Bill. 1994. Remarks on Signing the Social Security Independence and Program Improvement Act of 1994. White House: Washington, DC. August 15, 1994.

Clinton, Bill and Al Gore. 1992. *Putting People First: How We Can All Change America*. New York: Times Books.

Clinton, Bill and Al Gore. 1997. *The Blair House Papers*. Washington DC: National Performance Review.

Cohen, M.D., March, J. G., and Olsen. J. 1972. A Garbage Can Model of Organizational Choice. *Administrative Science Quarterly*. 17, 1-25.

Cohen, Wilber J. 1984. *Social Security Universal or Selective?*. Washington, DC: American Enterprise Institute for Public Policy Research.

Congressional Research Service. 1998a. *Social Security Financing and Taxation: Recent Issues: IP 435S*. Washington, DC: Congressional Research Services.

Congressional Research Service. 1998b. *Social Security: An Introduction*. Washington, DC: Congressional Research Service.

Contract With America Advancement Act. 1994. P.L. 104-121.

Coupland, Douglas. 1991. *Generation X*. New York: St. Martin Press.
Crozier, Michel. 1964. *The Bureaucratic Phenomenon*. Chicago: University of Chicago Press.

Dalber Financial Services, Inc. 1995. Press Release: Social Security Tops in Customer Service. May 3, 1995. Boston, Massachusetts: Dalber Financial Services, Inc.

Deal, T.E. and A. Kennedy. 1982. *Corporate Culture*. Reading, MA: Addison-Wesley Publishing.

Denhardt, Robert. 1981. *In the Shadow of Organizations*. Lawrence, KS: Regents Press of Kansas.

Dennison, D. R. 1990. *Corporate Culture and Organizational Effectiveness*. New York: John Wiley and Sons.

Derthick, Martha. 1979. *Policy Making for Social Security*. Washington, DC: Brookings Institution.

Downs, Anthony. 1967. *Inside Bureaucracy*. Boston: Little, Brown.

Driver, William J. 1985. "The Original Act was Just a Beginning" in *Social Security Act 50th Anniversary*. Baltimore: Social Security Administration.

Drucker, Peter F. 1985. *The Changing World of the Executive*. New York: Times Books.

Drucker, Peter F. 1986. *The Practice of Management*. New York: Harper & Row.

Drucker, Peter F. 1995a. *Managing in Time of Great Change*. New York Talley Books.

Drucker, Peter F. 1995b. Really Reinventing Government *The Atlantic Monthly*, February. pp. 65-67.

Eadie, Doughs. 1983. "Putting a Powerful Tool to Practical Use". *Public Administration Review*. 33:447-516.

Edwards, G. C. III. 1980. *Implementing Public Policy*. Washington, DC: Congressional Quarterly Press.

Eisner, Robert. 1998. *Social Security More, Not Less*. New York: The Century Foundation Press.

Elmore, R.F. 1985. *Forward and Backward Mapping: Reversible logic in the analysis of Public Policy*. pp. 33-70. In *Implementation in Federal and Unitary System*. K. Hanf & T.A.J. Toonen (Eds). Dordrecht: Martinus Nijhoff.

Epstein, Abraham. 1968. *A Challenge to America: A Study of Social Insurance in the US and Abroad*. New York: Agathan Press, Inc.

Executive Order No. 6757. 1934.Social Security in America. June 29.

Executive Order No. 12862. 1993. *Setting Customer Standards*. October 11.

Federickson, H. George. 1996. "Comparing the Reinventing Government Management with the New Public Administration". *Public Administration Review*. 56:263-270.

Galaskiewicz, J., and W. Bielefeld. 1998. *Nonprofit Organizations in an Age of Uncertainty: A study of Organizational Change*. New York: Aldine De Gruyter.

Galbraith, J. R. 1977. *Organization Design*. Reading, MA: Addison-Wesley.

Gargan, J.J. 1997. Reinventing Government and Reforming Public Administration. *International Journal of Public Administration*. 20: 221-247.

Gazell, J.A. 1997. "Ideological Reactions to the National Performance Review." *International Journal of Public Administration*. 20: 71-112.

General Accounting Office (GAO). 1987. *Administrative Leadership within the Social Security Administration*. GAO/HEHS-6789587. Washington, DC: General Accounting Office.

General Accounting Office (GAO). 1992. *Organizational Culture: Techniques Companies Use to Perpetuate or Change Beliefs and Values*. GAO/NSIAD-92-105. Washington, DC: General Accounting Office.

General Accounting Office (GAO). 1994a. *Government Performance and Results Act of 1993: An Executive's Guide*. Washington: General Accounting Office.

General Accounting Office (GAO). 1994b. *Management Reform: Implementation of the National Performance Review's Recommendation*. GAO/OCG-95-1. Washington, DC: General Accounting Office.

General Accounting Office (GAO). 1996a. *Effective Leadership Needed to Meet Challenges*. GAO/HEHS-969196. Washington, DC: General Accounting Office.
General Accounting Office (GAO). 1996b. *Management Reform: Completion Status of Agency Actions Under the National Performance Review*. GAO/GGD-96-94. Washington, DC: General Accounting Office.

General Accounting Office (GAO). 1996c. *Executive Guide: Effectively Implementing the Government Performance and Results Act*. GAO/GGD-96-118. Washington, DC: General Accounting Office.

General Accounting Office (GAO). 1996d. *Management Reform: Status of Agency Reinvention Lab Efforts*. GAO/GGD-96-69. Washington, DC: General Accounting Office.

General Accounting Office (GAO). 1997a. *The Government Performance and Results Act: 1997 Government Implementation will be Uneven*. GAO/GGD-97-109. Washington, DC: General Accounting Office.

General Accounting Office (GAO). 1997b. *GPRA: Managerial Accountability and Flexibility did not Work as Intended*. GAO/GCD-97-36. Washington, DC: General Accounting Office.

General Accounting Office (GAO). 1998. *Reinventing Government: Status of NPR Recommendations at 10 Federal Agencies*. GGD-10-145. Washington, DC: General Accounting Office.

General Accounting Office (GAO). 1999. *NPR's Savings- Claimed Agency Savings Cannot All be Attributed to NPR*. GAO/GGD-99-120. Washington, DC: General Accounting Office.

Glaser, Barney G. and Anselm L. Strauss. 1967. *The Discovery of Grounded Theory: Strategies for Qualitative Research*. Chicago: Aldine.

Goggins, M.L. 1986. The Too Few Cases to Many Variables: Problems in Implementation Research. *Western Political Quarterly*. 38: 328-347.

Goggins, Malcom, Ann Bowman, James Lester, and Lawrence O'Toole, Jr,. 1990. *Implementation Theory and Practice. Toward a Third Generation*. Glenview, IL:

Scott, Foresman, Little Brown.
Goleman, Daniel. 1998. "The Higher Mark: What Makes a Leader a Leader". *Harvard Business Review*. Nov-Dec., p. 94.

Golembiewski, R.T. 1972. *Renewing Organizations: The Laboratory Approach to Planned Change*. Itasca, IL: Peacock.

Golembiewski, R.T. 1997. As the NPR Twig was Bent: Objectives, Strategic Gaps, and Speculations. *International Journal of Public Administration*. 20: 139-187.

Goodsell, Charles T. 1993. Did NPR Reinvent Government Reform?. *The Public Manager*. 22: 7-11.

Gore, Al. 1993. *From Red Tape to Results Creating a Government that Works Better and Cost Less, the Report of the National Review*. New York: Penguin Group.

Gore, Al. 1994a. The New Job of the Federal Executive. *Public Administration Review*. 54: 317-321.

Gore, Al. 1994b. *Creating a Government That Works Better & Cost Less: Status Report*. Washington, DC: Government Printing Office.

Gore, Al. 1994c. *Putting Customers First: Standards for Serving the American People*. Washington, DC: Government Printing Office.

Gore, Al. 1995. *Common Sense Government Works Better and Cost Less Third Report of the NPR*. Washington DC: Government Printing Office.

Gore, Al. 1996. *Common Sense Government: Works Better and Cost Less: Final Report*. New York: Random House.

Gore, Al. 1997. *Business Like Government: Lessons Learned from America's Best Companies*. Washington DC: Government Printing Office.
Government Executive. 1999. "Energizer in Chief: NPR's Bob Stone". *Government Executive*. p. 13. December.

Graetz, Michael J. and Jerry L. Mashaw. 1999. *True Security: Rethinking American Social Insurance*. New York: Yale University Press.
Grafton, Carl. 1975. Creation of Federal Agencies. *Administration and Society*. 7: 328-65.

Grassley, Charles E. 1993. *The Heritage Lectures: Reinventing Government: The Final Verdict. Washington DC: The Heritage Foundation.*

Greiner, Larry E. 1967. Patterns of Organizational Change. *Harvard Business Review.* 45:119-131.

Gryski, Gerald. 1981. *Bureaucratic Policy Making in a Technological Society.* Mass: Schenkman Publishing Company.

Guest, Robert H. 1962. *Organizational Change: The Effect of Successful Leadership.* Homewood, IL: Dorsey Publishing.

Guy, Mary Ellen. 1997. (REGO) Reinventing Government Organizational Architecture, and Reality. *International Journal of Public Administration.* 20:113-138.

Haass, Richard N. 1999. *The Bureaucratic Entrepreneur: How to be Effective in any Unruly Organization.* Washington, DC: Brookings Institute Press.

Hage, Jerald. 1980. *Theories of Organization form, Process, and Transformation.* New York: Wiley.

Halachmi, Arie. 1991. *The Enduring challenge: Surviving and Excelling in a Changing World.* San Francisco: Jossey-Bass Publishers.

Harmon, Jeannette. 1997. *Basic Analyst Training: Social Security Administration Facts and Organizational Structure.* Atlanta, Georgia: Social Security Administration.

Hart, D.K. and D.W. Hart. 1997. Why the Gore Report Will Probably Fail. *International Journal of Public Administration.* 20: 183-220.

Harvey, Louis S. and Paul DiCesare. 1995. *World Class Benchmark: An Evaluation of Non-Financial Service Providers.* Washington DC: Dalbar, Inc.

Heclo, Hugh. 1977. *A Government of Strangers.* Washington, DC: Brooking Institution.

Hersey, Paul, and Kenneth H. Blanchard. 1993. *Management of Organizational Behavior: Utilizing Human Resources.* Englewood Cliffs, NJ: Prentice Hall.

Herzberg, Frederick. 1966. *Work and the Nature of Man.* New York: World.

Herzberg, Frederick, B. Mausner, and B. Snyderman. 1959. *Motivation to Work.* New York: John Wiley.

Holt, B.J. 1993. The Influences of State Government Agencies on the Implementation of Federal Programs: The Case of Aging Policy. *Dissertation Abstracts International.*

Holtzman, Abraham. 1965. *The Townsend Movement: A Political Study.* New York: Bookman Associates.

Hornstein, Harvey. 1971. *Social Intervention: A Behavior Science Approach.*
New York: MacMillan.

Human Development Council. 1997. *Getting Results through Learning.*
Washington, DC: Human Resource Development Council.
Ingram, H. 1980. Policy Implementation Thought Bargaining. *Public Policy.* 25: 499-526.

Ingraham, Patricia, James R. Thompson and Ronald P. Sanders, eds. 1998.
Transforming Forming Government. San Francisco: Jossey Bass.

Johnson, Janet and Richard Josylyn. 1986. *Political Science Research Methods.*
USA: Congressional Quarterly.

Kaiser, E.J. 1985. *Urban Land Use Planning.* Chicago: University of Illinois Press.

Kamensky, John M. 1996. Role of the 'Reinventing Government' movement in Federal
Management Reform. *Public Administration Review.* 56:247-255.

Kamensky, John. 1999. A Brief History: NPR. *Reinvention Express.* Retrieved from
http://www.npr.gov/whoweare/history2.html. May.

Kanter, B. 1995. *Understanding Capitalism: How Economies Work.* London: Boyars
Bowerdean.

Kanter, Rosabeth Moss. 1989. *When Giants Learn to Dance.* New York: Simon and
Schulster.

Kaufman, Herbert. 1960. *The Forest Ranger.* Baltimore, MD:
John Hopkins University Press.

Kaufman, Herbert. 1976. *Are Government Organizations Immortal?.* Washington:
Brookings Institution.

Kaufman, Herbert. 1981. *The Administrative Behavior of Federal Bureau Chiefs.*
Washington, DC: Brooking Institution.

Kaufman, Herbert. 1991. *Time, Change, and Organization: Natural Selection in a
Perilous Environment.* NJ: Chatham House Publishing.

Katz, D and Kahn, R.L. 1966. *The Social Psychology of Organization.*
New York: Willey.

Kettl, Donald F. 1994. *Reinventing Government? Appraising the National Performance
Review.* Washington DC: Brooking Institution.

Kettl, Donald F. and John Dilulio, Jr. 1995. *Inside the Reinvention Machine:
Appraising Reform.* Washington, DC: Brooking Institution.

Kilmann, Ralph H., Mary Saxton, and Roy Serpa.,eds. 1995. *Gaining Control of Corporate Culture.* San Francisco: Jossey-Bass.

Kingdon. John W. 1994. *Agendas, Alternatives, and Public Policy.* New York: Harper Collins.

Kingson, Eric R. and James H. Schulz. 1997. *Social Security in the 21st Century.* New York: Oxford Press.

Kimberly, J.C., R. Miles and Associates. 1980. *The Organizational Life Cycle Issues in the Creation, transformation, and Decline of Organizations.* San Francisco: Jossey-Bass.

Kingson, Eric R, and James H. Schulz. 1997. *Social Security in the 21st Century.* New York: Oxford University Press.

Koitz, David and Geoffrey Kollman. 1998. *Current Social Security Issues.* Washington, DC: Congressional Research Service.

Kouzes, James and Barry Posner. 1997. *The Leadership Challenge: How to get extraordinary things done in. Organizations.* San Francisco: Jossey-Bass Publications.

Lawrence, Paul R. 1958. *The Changing of Organizational Benefits Patterns: A Case Study of Decentralization.* Boston: Harvard Business School.

Lawrence, Paul and Lorsch, J.W. 1967. *Organization and Environment.* Cambridge, Mass: Harvard University Press.

Leavitt, Harold J. 1965. Applied Organizational Change in Industry: Structural, Technological and Humanistic Approaches. In James G. March (ed.), *Handbook of Organizations* (pp. 11-45). Chicago: Rand McNally and Company.

Lester, J.P. and Lombard. E.N. 1987. *Comparative State Environmental Policy: Toward An Intergovernmental Analysis.* Paper prepared for delivery at the annual meeting of the Southwest Political Science Association. Dallas, TX.

Lewin, Kurt. 1947. *The Research group for group dynamics.* New York: Beacon House.

Light, Paul. 1999. "Tallent Pool Runs Dry". *Government Executive.* p. 14. September.

Light, Paul. 2000. "Pressure to Grow: The next President Won't be able to keep a lid on the true size of Government". *Government Executive.* pp. 22-27.October.

Likert, R. 1961. *New Patterns of Management.* New York: McGraw-Hill.

Likert, R. 1967. *The Human Organization Its Management and Value.* New York: McGraw Hill.

Linder, S.H and Peters, B.G. 1987. "A Design Perspective on Policy Implementation: The Fallacies of Misplaced Prescriptions". *Policy Studies Review.* 6:459-475.

Lippitt, Gordon. 1969. *Organizational Renewal.* New York: Meredith Press.

Lippitt, Gordon. 1982. *A Holistic Approach to Organization Development, 2nd ed.* Englewood Cliff, NJ: Prentice-Hall.

Lipset, S.M. Trow, M. & Coleman J. 1962. *Union Democracy: The Inside Politics of the International Typographical Union.* New York: Macmillan.

Lipsky. Micheal. 1980. *The Street Level Bureaucracy.* New York: Sage Foundation.
Long, Huey. 1933. *The Autobiography of Huey P.Long.* New Orleans: National Books Co.

Lubove, Roy. 1968. *The Struggle for Security: 1900-1935.* Cambridge: Harvard University Press.

Luecke, Richard A. 1994. *Scuttle your Ships before Advancing and Other Lessons from History on Leadership and Change Today's Manager.* New York: Oxford University Press.

Luntz Research Company. 1994. *Social Security: The Credibility Gap- Summary of Results of September 8-10. Washington DC:* Luntz Research Company.

Lutrin, Carl and Shani, A.B. 1998. *Reinventing in the Public Sector: Some Lessons and Limits in Accountability and Radical Change in Public Organization.* Connecticut: Quorum Books.

Maccoby, Michael. 1976. *The Gamesman: the New Corporate Leaders.* New York: Simon and Schuster.

Machiavelli, Niccoló. 1961. Baltimore: Penguin Books.

Maisse, Joseph. 1965. Management Theory. In *Handbook of Organizations.* James March, ed., pp. 387-423. Chicago: Rand McNally.

March, J.G., and Simon, H.A. 1958. *Organizations.* New York: Wiley.

March, J.G. and Olsen J.P. 1989. *Rediscovering Institutions: The Organizational Basis of Politics.* New York: Free Press.

Maslow, Abraham. 1965. *Eusychian Management.* Homewood, IL: Richard D. Irwin.

Mayo, Elton. 1933. *The Human Problems of An Industrial Civilizations.* New York: MacMillian Co.

Mazmaniam, DA and Sabatier, P. 1983. *Can Regulation Work? The Implementation of the 1972 California Costal Iniative.* New York: Plenna Press.

McCracken, Grant. 1988. *The Long Interview*. Newbury Park, CA: Sage Publications, Inc.

McKinley, Charles, Frase, Robert W. 1970. *Launching Social Security:*
A Capture and Record Account 1935-37. Madison: The University of Wisconsin.

McGregor, Douglas. 1960. *The Human Side of Enterprise*. New York: McGraw-Hill
Book Company.

McGregor, Douglas. 1966. *Leadership and Motivation*. Massachusetts: M.I.T.

Meyer, M.W. 1978. *Environments and Organizations*. San Francisco: Jossey-Bass.

Meyer, M.W. 1979. *Change in Public Bureaucracies*. London: Cambridge University
Press.

Meyers, Robert J. 1993. *Social Security 4th ed*. Philadelphia, Penn:
University of Penn Press.

Mintzberg, Henry. 1979. *The Structuring of Organizations*. Chicago:
University of Chicago Press.

Moe, Ronald. 1994. The Reinventing Government Exercise: Misinterpreting the Problem,

Misjudging the Consequences. *Public Administration Review*. 54:111-122.

Montjoy, R.S. and L.J. O'Toole. 1979. Toward a Theory of Policy Implementation an
Organizational Perspective. *Public Administration Review*. 39: 465-476.

Morgan, Gareth. 1986. *Images of Organizations*. Newbury, California:
Sage Publications, Inc.

Morse, Nancy and Reimer E. 1956. The Experimental Change of a Major Organizational
Variable". *Journal of Abnormal Social Psychology*. 52: 120-29.

Myers, Robert J. 1993. *Social Security, 4th ed*. Philadelphia, Penn:
University of Pennsylvania Press.

Nachimia, Chava Frankfort and David Nachmias. 1992. *Research Methods in the Social*
Sciences. New York: St. Martin's Press.

Nalbandian, J., and J.T. Edwards. 1983. "The Professional Values of Public
Administrators: A Comparison with Lawyers, Social Workers, and Business
Administration. *Review of Public Personnel Administration*. 4:1-11.

Nash, Gerald, Noel H. Pugash, and Richard F. Tomasson. 1988. *Social Security: The*
First Half of the Century. Albuquerque NM: University of New Mexico Press.

Neustadt, Richard E. 1960. Presidential Powers: Politics of Leadership. New York: Wiley.

Neustadt, Richard E and Earnest R. May. 1986. *Thinking in Time: The Uses of History for Decision Makers*. New York: The Free Press.

Norris, Michael E. 2000. *Reinventing the Administrative State*. Maryland: University Press of America.

National Performance Review (NPR). 1995. *Putting Customers First Securing the American Public: Best Practices in Telephone Service*. Washington DC: Government Printing Office.

National Performance Review (NPR). 1996. *Blair House Papers*. Washington DC: Government Printing Office.

Oasis. 1997a. Employees contribute to world-class-service standards. *Oasis*, p 13. September

Oasis. 1997b. Reinvention: Improving Service to Our Customer. *Oasis*. pp 5-8. August.

Ocala, Florida, Manager's Presentation Report. 1998. Atlanta, Georgia. January 7.

O'Neill, Tip. 1987. *Man of the House: The Life and Political Memoirs of Speaker Tip O'Neill*. New York: Random House.

Osborne, David and Peter Plastrick. 1997. *Banishing Bureaucracy: The Five Strategies for Reinventing Government*. Mass: Addison-Wesley Publishing Company.

Osborne, David and Ted Gabler. 1993. *Reinventing Government: How the Entrepreneurial Spirit is Transforming the Public Sector*. Mass: Penguin Books.

O'Sullivan, Elizabethann and Gary R. Rassel. 1995. *Research Methods for Public Administrators*. New York: Longman.

O'Toole, James. 1995. *Leading Change: Overcoming the Ideology of Comfort and the Tyranny of Custom*. San Francisco: Jossey-Bass Publishers.

O'Toole, L. J. 1986. "Policy Recommendation for Multi Actor Implementation: An Assessment of the field". *Journal of Public Policy*. 6: 181-210.

O'Toole, L.J. and Montjoy, Robert. 1984. Interorganizational Policy Implementation: A Theoretical Perspective. *Public Administration Review*. 44:491-503.

Ott, Steven. 1989. *The Organization Culture Perspective*. Chicago, IL: The Dorsey Press.

Ouchi, W. 1981. *Theory Z: How American Business Can Meet The Japanese Challenge*. Reading Mass: Addison-Wesley Publishing Company.

171

Palumbo, D.J. & Calista, D.J. 1990. *Implementation and the Policy Process: Opening the Black Box.* New York: Greenwood Press.

Paulos, Jose. 1996. *Service is My Job.* Miami, Florida: Social Security Administration.

Perry, J.L. and L.W. Porter. 1982. "Factors Affecting the Context for Motivation in Public Organizations." *Academy of Management Review,* 7:82-89.

Perry, J.L. and L.R. Wise. 1990. "The Motivation Base of Pubic Service." *Public Administration Review.* 50:367-373.

Peters, B. Guy and Donald Savoie. 1995. *Governance in a Changing Environment.* Canada: Canadian Center for Management Development.

Peters, Tom and R.H. Waterman. 1982. *In Search of Excellence: Lessons from America's Best Run Companies.* New York: Harper & Row.

Peterson, Peter G. 1996. *Will America Grow Up Before it Grows Old?* New York: Random House.

Pfiffner, JP. 1997. The National Performance Review in Perspective. *International Journal of Public Administration.* 20:41-70.

Poister, Theodore and Gregory Streib. 1994. Municipal Management Tools from 1976 to 1993: An Overview and Update. *Public Productivity and Management Review.* 18: 115-125.

Ponnuru, Ramesh. 1997. "Securing Social Security: Ponzi's Revenge". *National Review.* February 24.

Poole, Marshall Scott, Andrew H. Van de Ven, Kevin Dooley, and Michael E. Holmes. *Organizational Change and Innovation Processes.* New York: Oxford Press.

Pressman, Jeffrey L. and Aaron Wildavsky. 1973. *Implementation: How Great Expectations in Washington are Dashed in Oakland.* Berkley, CA: Univ of CA Press.

Quinn, R.E. and Cameron K. 1983. Organizational Life Cycles and Shifting Criteria of Effectiveness: Some Preliminary Evidence. *Management Science.* 29: 33-51.

Rainey, Hal. 1991. *Understanding and Managing Public Organizations.* San Francisco: Jossey Bass.

Rainey, Hal G., Robert W. Backoff, and Charles H. Levine. 1976. Comparing Public and Private Organizations. *Public Administration Review.* 36:233-37.

Rawls, J.R., R.A. Ullrich, and O.T. Nelson. 1975. "A Comparison of Mangers Entering or Reentering the Profit and Nonprofit Sectors". *Academy of Management Journal.* 18:616-622.

Reich, Robert. 1987. *Tales of a New America: the Anxious Liberal Guide to the Future*. New York: Vintage Books.

Reich, Robert. 1997. *Locked in the Cabinet*. New York: Alfred Knopf.

Reich, Robert. 2000. *Success at Work*. New York: Alfred Knopf.
"Reinventing what?". 1999. *Atlanta Journal and Constitution*. October 6. A 6.

Rivlin, Alice. 1994. Speech to NPR conference. Atlanta, Georgia. April 5, 1994.

Rogers, Robert W., John W. Hayden, B. Jean Ferketish, and Robert Matzen. 1995. *Organizational Change That Works: How to Merge Culture and Business Strategies for Maximum Results*. Pennsylvania: DDI Press.

Rohr, John. A. 1986. *To Run a Constitution: The Legitimacy of the Administrative State*. Lawrence, KS: University of Kansas.

Roosevelt, Franklin. 1934. *Public Papers and Addresses of Franklin Delanor Roosevelt*. Washington, DC. Government Printing Office.

Roosevelt, Franklin. 1935. *Public Papers and Addresses of Franklin Delanor Roosevelt*. Washington, DC: Government Printing Office.

Rosenbloon, David H. and James D. Carroll. 1990. *Toward Constitution Competence: A Casebook for Public Administration*. New Jersey: Prentice Hall.

Rubinow, I.M. 1934. *The Quest for Security*. New York: Henry Holt and Company.
Sabatier, P.A. 1986. Top-Down and Bottom Up Approaches to Implementation Research: A Critical Analysis and Suggested Synthesis. *Journal of Public Policy*. 15:21-48.

Sabatier, P.A. and Mazmanian. 1980. Policy Implementation: A Framework of Analysis. *Policy Studies*. 8: 536-560.

Saldarini, Katy. 1999. Reinvention Report Card. *Government Executive*. p 6. October.

Sayles, Leonard. 1962. Change Process in Organizations: An Applied Anthropological Analysis. *Human Organizations*. 21:62-67.

Schein, E.H. 1981. *Organizational Psychology*. (3rd. Ed.) Englewood Cliffs, NJ: Prentice-Hall.

Schein, E.H. 1984. Coming to a New Awareness of Organizational Culture. *Sloan Management Review*. 25: 3-16.

Schein, E.H. 1985. *Organizational Culture and Leadership*. San Francisco, CA: Jossey-Bass Publishers.

Schieber, Sylvester J. and John B. Shoven. 1999. *The Real Deal*. New York: Vall-Ballow Press.

Selznick, Philip. 1957. *Leadership in Administration: a Sociological Interpretation*. New York, Harper & Row.

Senge, Peter. 1995. *The Fifth Discipline*. New York: Currency Double Day.

Sergiovanni, Thomas J. and John E. Corbally. 1984. *Leadership and Organizational Culture: New Perspective on Administrative Theory and Practice*. Urbana: University of Illinois Press.

Seymour, Martin Lipsett, Martin Trow, and James Coleman. 1962. *Union Democracy*. Garden City, NJ: Anchor Publishing.

Shepard, Herbert. 1965. "Changing Interpersonal and Inter-Group Relationships in Organizations", In *Handbook of Organizations*. James March, ed. Pp. 1115-1144. Chicago: Rand McNally.

Sherman, Gordon. 1994. Speech to Managers Regional Meeting. Atlanta, Georgia. August 10, 1994.

Sherman, Gordon. 1998. Social Security: The Real Story. *Phi Kappa Phi Journal*. Spring 1998.

Sherman, Gordon. 1999. On Leadership. Paper presented at the meeting of the Federal Southeastern Recruiting Conference, Fort Lauderdale, Florida. August 25.

Shuy, Roger W. 1998. *Bureaucratic Language*. Washington, DC: Georgetown University Press.

Social Security Act of 1935, 49 Stat., 620.

Social Security Independence and Program Improvement Act of 1994. P.L. 103-296.

Social Security Administration (SSA). 1975. *Master Plan for Development for the Development of the future of the Social Security Process*. Baltimore: Social Security Administration.

Social Security Administration (SSA). 1988. *Social Security 2000: A Strategic Plan*. Baltimore: Social Security Administration.

Social Security Administration (SSA). 1991. *The Social Security Plan: A Framework for the Future*. Baltimore: Social Security Administration.

Social Security Administration (SSA). 1995a. *Social Security Bulletin: 50th Anniversary Issue*. 48:8. Washington DC: Social Security Administration.

Social Security Administration (SSA). 1995b. *Red Book on Work Incentives*. Washington DC: SSA pub 436900.

Social Security Administration (SSA). 1995c. *The Business Plan*. Baltimore: Social Security Administration.

Social Security Administration (SSA). 1996. Award Program. Atlanta, GA: Social Security Administration.
Social Security Administration (SSA). 1997. *Human Resource*. Baltimore: Social Security Administration.

Social Security Administration (SSA). 1998a. *Brief History of Social Security*. Baltimore: Social Security Administration.

Social Security Administration (SSA). 1998b. *Social Security Update 1998: SSA Publication 05-10003*. Washington DC: US Government Printing Office.

Social Security Administration (SSA). 1998c. *Ambassador Program: Friends and Neighbors Session*. Baltimore, MD: Social Security Administration.

Social Security Administration (SSA). 1998d. *Social Security Basic Facts*. Baltimore: Social Security Administration.

Social Security Administration (SSA). 1998e. *Social Security Handbook*. Baltimore: Social Security Administration.

Social Security Administration (SSA). 1998f. *Social Security: Understanding the Benefits*. Baltimore: Social Security Administration.

Social Security Administration (SSA). 1998e. *Internal Report: Perspectives of the Atlanta Region*. Baltimore: Social Security Administration.

Social Security Administration (SSA). 2000a. *Social Security*. Baltimore: Social Security Administration

Social Security Administration (SSA). 2000b. *Social Security Business Plan*. Baltimore: Social Security Administration.

Stake, Robert. 1995. *The Art of Case Study Research*. Thousand Oaks, CA: Sage Publications.

Stewart, Debra and G. David Garson. 1983. *Organizational Behavior and Management*. New York: Marcel Dekker.

Stogdill, R.M. 1974. *Handbook of Leadership*. New York: Free Press.

Stone, Bob. 1994. Speech to NPR conference. Atlanta, Georgia. April 5, 1994.

Strauss, George. 1964. *Some Notes on Power Equalization*. Berkeley: University of California Press.

Sweeny, Jenne C. and Hyde, AC. 1995. Public Manager 1995 Annual Survey. *The Public Manager.* Pp. 56-64.

Tead, Ordway. 1935. *The Art of Leadership.* New York: McGraw Book Company, Inc.

Terreberry, Shirley. 1968. The Evolution of Organizational Environments. *Administrative Science Quarterly.* 12: 590-613.

The Atlanta Region Center for Human Resources. 1997. *Continuing to Provide World Class Service.* Atlanta, GA: author.

Thompson, James. 1967. *Organizations in Action.* New York: McGraw-Hill.

Thompson, Joe. 1996. "Process reviews will provide answers: What's Really Happening out there? And what needs to be done?". *Oasis.* p. 6. August.

Thompson, Lawrence. 1994. Speech to SSA Managerial Conference. August 10, 1994.

Thompson, Victor A. 1969. *Bureaucracy and Innovation.* Tuscalloosa, AL: Univesity of Alabama Press.

Toynbee, Arnold J. 1947. *A Study of History.* New York: Oxford University Press.

Tushman, Michael. 1974. *Organizational Change: An Explanatory Study and Case History.* New York: Cornell University.

Tynes, Sheryl. 1996. *Turning Points in Social Security: from 'Cruex Hoax' to Sacred Entitlement.* Stanford, CA: Stanford University Press.

Utterback, J.M. 1994. *Mastering the Dynamics of Innovation: How Companies Seize Opportunities in the Face of Technological Change.* Boston: Harvard Business School Press.

Waldo, Dwight. 1978. Organizing Theory Revisiting the Elephant, *Public Administration Review.* 32: 589-597.

Walker, David B. 1996. "The Advent of an Ambiguous Federalism and the Emergence of the New Federalism." *Public Administration Review.* 56: 271-280.

Walker, David M. 1997. *Retirement Security: Understanding and Planning Your Financial Future.* New York: John Wiley & Sons, Inc.

Wall Street Journal. 1993. "Al Gore's Right Track". *Wall Street Journal.* 3 Sept 1993. A8:col 3.

Warrick, Don. 1984. *Managing Organizational Change and Development.* Washington DC: Library of Congress.

Washington Post. 1993. "From Camelot to Clinton: A Statistical Portrait of the US". August 23 1993. A15.

Weber, M. 1946. *From Max Weber: Essays in Sociology.* Translated: edited by H.H. Gerth and C. Wright Mills. New York: Oxford University Press.

Weber, Max. 1968. *On Charisma and Industrial Building.* Chicago: The University of Chicago Press.
Weick, Karl. 1968. *The Social Psychology of Organizing, 2nd ed.* Reading Mass: Addison Wesley Publications.

Weinberg, M.W. 1983. Public Management and Private Management: A Diminishing Gap?. *Journal of Policy Analysis and Management.* 3:107-125.

White, Jay D. 1997. The Unconscious Life of Organizations. *Public Administration Review.* 57:358-359.

Wilson, James Q. 1989. *Bureaucracy: What Government Agencies Do and Why They do it.* New York: Basic Books.

Wilson, James Q. 1994. Reinventing PA. John Gaus Lecture at 1994 APSA Convention. NYC. 25.

Wilson, Woodrow. 1885. *Congressional Governing: A Study in American Politics.* New York: Houghton, Mifflin and Company.

Wilson, Woodrow. 1887. "The Study of Administration". *Political Science Quarterly.* Reprinted in Jay M. Shfritz and Albert Hyde 1987 *Classics of Public Administration.* , 2nd ed. Chicago: Dorsey Press. pp. 10-25

Witte, Edwin E. 1955. *Reflections on the Beginning of Social Security.* Baltimore: Social Security Pub. NO. 87-72. 11-72.

Witte, Edwin E. 1962. *The development of the Social Security Act.* Madison: University of Wisconsin Press.

Wittrock, B. and Deleon. 1986. "Policy as a Moving Target: A target for Conceptual Realism". *Policy Studies Review.* 6:44-60.

Woodward, J. 1965. *Industrial Organization: Theory and Practice.* London: Oxford University Press.

Woodward, Richard W. and William A. Pasmore. 1987. *Research in Organizational Change & Development.* Greenwhich, Conn: JAI Press, Inc.

Wright, Jim. 1996. *Balancing of Power: Presidents and Congress from the Era of McCarthy to the Age of Gringrich.* Atlanta: Turner Publishing, Inc.

Van de Ven, Andrew, and Ferry Diane. 1981. *Measuring and Assessing Organization.* New York: Wiley Interscience.

Van Meter, Donald and Van Horn, Carl. 1975. The Implementation Process: A Conceptual Framework. *Administration and Society*. 6: 445-488.

Vecchio, Robert. 1988. *Organizational Behavior*. Chicago, IL: Dryden Press.

Yin, Robert K. 1993. *Applications of Case Study Research*. Newbury Park, CA: Sage Publications, Inc.

Yin, Robert K. 1989. *Case Study Research: Design and Methods*, Newbury Park, CA: Sage Publications, Inc.

Yoder, Eric. 2001. Agency Focus: Overload at the Social Security Administration. *Government Executive*, pp. 7-14. September.

Yukl, Gary A. 1981. *Leadership in Organization*. New Jersey: Prentice Hall.

Zaltman, Gerald, Robert Duncan, and Johnny Holbeck. 1977. *Strategies for Planned Change*. New York: Wiley.

Zaleznick, Abraham. 1964. Interpersonal Relationships in Organizations. In Handbook of Organizations, James March, ed., pp. 574-614. Chicago: Rand McNally.

Interviews

Barrera, Francisco (Chic). 1996. Assistant Regional Commissioner for Management and Operations Support (ARC-MOS) for the Southern Region. Interview with author. Atlanta, Georgia. June 13, 1996

Barrera, Francisco (Chic). 1997. Assistant Regional Commissioner for Management and Operations Support (ARC-MOS) for the Southern Region. Interview with author. Atlanta, Georgia. June 30, 1997

Brown, Jimmy. 1998. Field Office Manager for the Opelika, Alabama office. Interview with author. Opelika, Alabama. June 3, 1998.

Bunton, Willett. 1998. NPR Staff member. Interview with author. Juniper Beach, Florida. August 9, 1998.

Carter, Sola Felicitia (Feli). 1997. Director of Training, previously on NPR implementation project. Interview with author. SSA headquarters, Baltimore, Maryland.

Chater, Shirley. 1996. SSA Commissioner . Interview with author. Atlanta, Georgia. June 24, 1996.

Chater, Shirley. 1997. SSA Commissioner . Interview with author. Atlanta, Georgia. April 14, 1997.

Chater, Shirley. 1997. SSA Commissioner . Interview with author. Auburn, Alabama. April 15, 1997.

Chlumsky, John. 1997. Director of Policy Net. Interview with author. SSA headquarters, Baltimore, Maryland. September 8, 1997.

Colvin, Carolyn. 1997. Deputy Commissioner for Programs and Policy. Interview with author. SSA Headquarters, Baltimore, Maryland. September 9, 1997.

Dewitt, Larry. 1997. SSA Historian. Interview with author. SSA Headquarters, Baltimore, Maryland. September 8, 1997.

Fairbrother, Doug. 1997. NPR Team Member. Interview with author. NPR Headquarters, Washington, DC. September 10, 1997.

Fine, Hal. 1997. Deputy Regional Commissioner for the Southern Region. Interview with author. Atlanta, Georgia. July 22, 1996.

Fine, Hal. 1998. Deputy Regional Commissioner for the Southern Region. Interview with author. Atlanta, Georgia. June 30, 1998.

Flavin, Tom. 1997. NPR Staff member. Interview with author. NPR headquarters, Washington, DC. September 10, 1997.

Gracie, Pat. 1997. Commissioner's Executive Staff member and Strategic Management director. Interview with author. SSA Headquarters, Baltimore, Maryland. September 9, 1997.

Harmon, Jeannette. 1996. Executive Office for the Southern Region of SSA. Interview with author. Atlanta, Georgia. June 12, 1996.

Kamensky, Greg. 1997. NPR Deputy Director. Interview with author. NPR Offices, Washington, DC. September 10, 1997.

Kane, Candy. 1997. NPR Staff member. Interview with author. NPR Offices, Washington, DC. September 10, 1997.

Lelane, Toni. 1996. SSA's Chief Policy Officer for NPR. Interview with author. Atlanta, Georgia. June 17, 1996.

Lelane, Toni. 1997. SSA's Chief Policy Officer for NPR. Interview with author. SSA headquarters, Baltimore, Maryland. September 9, 1997.

Marshall, Kurt. 1997. NPR staff member focused on Government and Performance Act of 1993 (GPRA) implementation. Interview with author. NPR headquarters, Washington, DC. September 10, 1997.

Morris, Tommy. 1996. Georgia State Director. Interview with Author. Atlanta, Georgia. September 9, 1996.

Patterson, Patty. 1998. Deputy Public Affairs Officer. Interview with author. Atlanta, Georgia. July 16, 1998.

Sherin-Jones, Carolyn. 1997. Director of Strategic Management and Planning. Interview with author. SSA headquarters, Baltimore, Maryland. September 9, 1997.

Sherman, Gordon. 1996. Southern Regional Commissioner for SSA. Interview with the author. Atlanta, Georgia. August 7, 1996.

Sherman, Gordon. 1996a. Southern Regional Commissioner for SSA. Interview with the author. Atlanta, Georgia. June 15, 1997.

Shiply, Tom. 1997. Strategic Planning staff member. Interview with author. SSA Headquarter. Baltimore, Maryland. September 8, 1997.

Spearman, Theresa. 1996. Human Resource Director for the Southern Region of SSA. Interview with author. Atlanta, Georgia. June 20, 1996.

Spencer, Pete. 1997. Deputy Regional Commissioner for the San Francisco Region. I Interview with author. Atlanta, Georgia. June 19, 1997.

Torrado, Miguel. 1997. Director of Civil Rights and Equal Opportunity Office (CREO). Interview with author. SSA Headquarters. Baltimore, Maryland. September 8, 1997.

Walker, David. 1998. Comptroller General and director of the General Accounting Office. General Accounting Office headquarters. Washington, DC. February 8, 1998.

Walker, David. 1999. General Accounting Office Comptroller. Personal Interview. GAO headquarters, Washington, DC. May 7, 1999.

Woods, Greg. NPR Deputy Director. Interview with author. NPR headquarters. Washington, DC. September 10, 1997.

Warden, Janice. 1997. Deputy Commissioner for Operations. Interview with author. SSA Atlanta, Georgia. April, 21, 1997.

Walker, Linda. 1997. Southeastern Director for NPR. Interview with author. Summit Building, Atlanta, Georgia. August 17, 1997.

Wilson, Quittie. 1996. Director of the Program Service Center. Interview with author. Birmingham, Alabama. August 26, 1997.

Memoranda American Federation of Government Employees AFL-CIO (AFGE). Internal Notes from meeting held on June 10-12, 1996. Atlanta. Georgia.

Carter, Jimmy. April 19, 1994. Letter To Vice President Al Gore, re: Georgia Common Access.

Chater, Shirley. March 10, 1995. Memo to Staff. Re: REGO Report.
Clinton, Bill. March 22, 1995. White House Memo re: Customer Service Standards.
Dyer, John. April 30, 1996. Memo about Agency Performance Methods.

Eisenger, Richard A. September 21, 1992. internal memo.

Gore, Al. April 29, 1993. Letter to former President Jimmy Carter, response to his April 19, 1993 letter.

Gore, Al. June 21, 1996. E-mail re: Opening of the Atlanta one-stop General Store.

Pat Gracie. July 7, 1997. Commissioner's Executive Staff member and Strategic Management director. Electronic Mail to author.

Gracie, Pat. September 8, 1997. Commissioner's Executive Staff member and Strategic Management director. Notes given to author from speech to Managers meeting conference. Baltimore, Maryland.

Harmon, Jeannette. February 2, 1997a. Internal memo with summary of executive staff meeting notes.

Harmon, Jeannette. July 30, 1997b. Internal memo with summary of executive staff meeting notes.

Harmon, Jeannette. August 5, 1997c. Internal memo with summary of executive staff meeting notes.

Harmon, Jeannette. August 9, 1997d. Internal memo with executive staff note.

Harmon, Jeanette. April 3, 1998. Internal memo.

Ponder, Fred. June 13, 1997. Internal Memo to all SSA State Directors, State DDS Administrators in the Atlanta Region.

Sherman, Gordon. February 11, 1997. Internal Memo to staff summarizing key action items from Executive Off-Site Meeting.

Taylor, Rodney. June 20, 1997. Internal Memo to Regional Commissioner.

Warden, Janice. December 19, 1996. Acting Deputy Commissioner for Human Resources. Memorandum to all Regional Commissioners, Restructuring of Field Organization and Upgrade of Field Management Positions".

Appendix A Structured Interview

APPENDIX A: The Questions Used in the Structured Interviews and were modified according to interviewee, SSA, NPR, etc.

1. What is your background in the Social Security Administration and current responsibilities?
   1.1. Gender
   1.2. Race
   1.3. Education
   1.4. Employment history
   1.5. Length of employment
   1.6. Length of employment in current position
2. How is policy developed in SSA?
3. Leadership
   3.1. How is leadership in the organization derived?
4. Change
   4.1. How has the organization adapted to change?
5. Culture
   5.1. Inquires about artifacts, values, and assumptions
6. Organizational mission
   6.1. What does the Social Security Administration do and how was the planning process developed?
   6.2. How do you measure these objectives to the lowest level within the organization? For example, in Opelika, Alabama.
7. Policy Implications
   7.1. What are the policy implications of NPR?
   7.2. What are the policy implications of the GPRA (1993 Government Performance Results Act)?

Appendix B Internal Memo with Agency Acronyms

ACRONYMS

Positions

AA	Administrative Aide
AAA	Area Administrative Assistant
AD	Area Director
ADO	Area Directors Office
ADM	Assistant District Manager {BM}
AU	Administrative Law Judge
AMM	Assistant Module Manager
AQ	Adjudication Officer
ARC	Assistant Regional Commissioner
ASC	Area Systems Coordinator
BA	Benefit Authorizer
BAI	Benefit Authorizer Intern
BC	Branch Chief
CA	Claims Authorizer
CATA (CTA)	Claims Authorizer Technical Assistant
CC	Claims Clerk
CCRE	Claims, Check and Remittance Examiner
CR	Claims Representative
CREOM Manager	Civil Rights and Equal Opportunity
CR-Tll	Claims Representative Title 2
CRTXVI	Claims Representative Title 16
CRT	Claims Representative Trainee
CRT	Claims Record Technician
CS	Contact Specialist
CSS	Claims Support Specialist
DARC	Deputy Assistant Regional Commissioner
DC	Disability Consultant
DCM	Disability Claims Manager
DCR	Debtor Contact Representative
DCO District Manager	Deputy Commissioner for Operations
DRC	Deputy Regional Commissioner
DRT	Data Review Technician
DS	Debt Specialist
EA	Executive Assistant
FR	Field Representative
F0 Field Office	
FOAM	Field Office Assistant Manager
FOM	Field Office Manager
IES	Inquiry and Expediting Specialist
MCL	Manager Class Leader
MM	Module Manager
MSS	Management Support Specialist
OM	Operations Manager
OMNI	Omnibuis {typist-data entry position)

OS	Operations Supervisor
OB	Operations Support Branch
PETE	Post Entitlement Technical Expert
RC	Regional Commissioner
RPAO	Regional Public Affairs Officer
RR	Reconsideration Reviewer
SLC	Site LAN Coordinator Service Representative
STC	Site Training Caordinator
SYSCO	Systems Coordinator
TA	Technical Assistant {Field Office)
TL	Team Leader
TSCOM	Teleservice Center Operations Manager
TSR	Teleservice Representative

Procedures/Manuals

AIMS	Administrative Instructions Manual System
CMM	Correspondence Manager Manual
SAM	General Administration Manual
MIM	Management Information Manual
MRM	Material Resources Manual
MSOM	Modernized System Operations Manual
PMS	Personnel Manual for Supervisors
POMS	Program Operations Manual Systems
ROTS	Receiving Office Training Guide
TSCOG	Teleservice Center Operations Guide

COMMONLY USED SSA ACRONYMS NEW & OLD

Organizational Components

BP&P	Benefits, Processing & Payroll
CABT	Contract Administration and Benefit Team {CABS)
CASLI	Cooperative Administrative Support Unit
CDO	Center for Disability Operations
CFPM	Center for Fiscal & Property Management
CHR	Center for Human Resources
CO	Central Office
COS	Center for Operations Support
COU	Computer Operations Unit
CPM	Classification & Position Management
CRED	Civil Rights & Equal Opportunity Staff (EEO) (also Diversity and Equal Opportunity—DEO)
DDS	Disability Determinations Service
DO	District Office
DOC	Data Operations Center
DMS	Debt Management Section
DPOC	Disability Program Operations Center {DPBIDPS)
DOB	Disability Quality Branch

DRS	Disability Review Section
FMT	Financial Management Team (FMS)
FST	Field Services Team
FO	Field Office
FT	Facilities Team (FS}
GPO	Government Printing Office
GSA	General Services Administration
KCFA	Health Care Financing Administration
HHS	Health and Human Services
HRC	Human Resources Center {HRB}
IEU	Inquiry & Expediting Unit
IPT	Insurance Program Team
LMERT	Labor Relations & Employee Relations Team
MAPT	Management Analysis Policy Team
MAST	Mainframe Application Support Team
MIOAT	Management Information & Office Automation Team
MOS	Management and Operations Support
(M&B *I* P05)	
NRC	Nations Records Center {CFS}
OAS	Operations Analysis Section
OCRO	Office of Central Records Operations
ODIO	Office of Disability & International Operations
OSC	Office of the General Counsel
OHA	Office of Hearings and Appeals
OIG	Office of Inspector General
OMB	Operations Management Staff
ORC	Office of the Regional Commissioner
ORPA	Office of Regional Public Affairs
ORQA	Office of Regional Quality Assurance

OSB Operation Support Branch

osc	Office Service Center {OSPC}
OSPB	Office Services and Planning Branch
PAT	Personnel Administration Team (PAS)
PCO	Processing Center Operations
PCST	Personal Computer Support Team

Organizational Components

poc	Program Operations Center {IIAPB *IAPSI* PS)
POT	Personnel Operations Team
PT	Procurement Team {PS}
PSC	Program Service Center
RASC	Regional Administrative Support Center
RCIU	Regional Commissioner's Inquiries Unit
RECON	Reconsideration
RO	Regional Office
S&P	Staffing & Placement
SDT	State Director's Office (ADO—Area Directors Office>
SOT	Software Development Team
SIT	Security and Integrity Team

SOST	System Operations Support Team
SPC	Statistical Process Control
SPT	Statistical Program Team
SPOC	Systems & Programs Operations Center {SSAB}
SSA	Social Security Administration
TSC	Teleservice Center
TEDT	Training and Employee Development Team (TED)
TII	Title 2 (same as T2 and RSOI>
TTS	Technical Training Staff
TXVI	Title 16 (same as T16 and SSI)
VIS	Visual Information Staff
VR	Vocational Rehabilitation

System Related

BLU	Basic LAN User Training
ABC	Automated Budget Control
BCC	Blind Courtesy Copy
CC	Courtesy Copy
CCCS	Commissioner's Correspondence Control System
DOS	Disk Operating System
FOSE	Field Office Systems Enhancement
IWS/LAN	Intelligent Workstation Local Area Network
LAN	Local Area Network
MCS	Modernized Claims System
MSSICS	Modernized Supplemental Security Income Claims System
PC	Personal Computer
PC	Program Circular
PCACS	Program Center Action Control System
SSADARS	Social Security Administration Data Acquisition and Retrieval System
TMP	Travel Manager Plus Other
AH	Account Holder
AL	Annual Leave
AN	Account Number
ARM	Atlanta Regional Memorandum
BAIP	Benefit Authorizer Intern Program
COB	Close of Business
CPI	Character Per Inch
DCU	Data Communication Utility
DI	Department of Interior
EEO	Equal Employment Opportunity
FPPS	Federal Personnel & Payment System
FY	Fiscal Year
FYI	For Your Information
ICN	Internal Control Number
IRD	Intercom anent Review Draft
MOEP	Metropolitan Office Enhancement Project
MPO	Model Paperless Office
MOU	Memorandum of Understanding
MTAS	Mainframe Time & Attendance System
NL	Notice Language
NPR	National Performance Review
OJT	On-the-Job Training

OASDI	Old Age, Survivor, Disability Insurance
OPM	Office of Personnel Management
PC	Program Circular
PCD	Pre-Clearance Date
PEBES	Personal Earnings and BenefIt Estimate Statement
PI	Public information Presidential Intern
RIC	Report of Contact
RDSHI	Retirement, Survivors Disability, and Health Insurance
RSI	Retirement & Survivors Insurance
SL	Sick Leave
SSI	Supplemental Security Income
STAR	Special Terminal and Adaptive Resources

About the Author

Dr. Wilson L. Triviño is a speaker, writer, and futurist. He resides in Atlanta, Georgia.

If you would like to interview Dr. Triviño, book to speak at your next event, or review a product or a cool social occasion, contact him at Twitter / Instagram @abcvision or abcvision@hotmail.com

www.ingramcontent.com/pod-product-compliance
Lightning Source LLC
Chambersburg PA
CBHW001150270320
41930CB00014B/3104